RAPCORE
The Nu-Metal Rap Fusion

Dick Porter

Plexus, London

Copyright © 2003 by Dick Porter
Published by Plexus Publishing Limited
55a Clapham Common Southside
London SW4 9BX
First printing 2003
www.plexusbooks.com

British Library Cataloguing in Publication Data

Porter, Dick
    Rapcore : the nu-metal rap fusion
    1. Rap (Music)
    I. Title
    782.4'2'1649

    ISBN 085965 321 8

Cover design by Phil Gambrill
Cover photograph by Paul Bergen, Redferns
Printed and bound in Spain by Bookprint S.L, Barcelona

It has not been possible in all cases to trace the
copyright sources, and the publishers would be glad
to hear from any such unacknowledged copyright holders.

CONTENTS

INTRODUCTION
(Not) Defining a Genre

Nu-metal is a subjective concept, the definition of which varies depending upon whom you talk to. Fans of particular acts will argue long and hard about what constitutes nu-metal, rap-metal, rapcore, alt-metal, or such esoteric sub-genres as technical metal and grindcore. Everyone will formulate their own hierarchy of fusion styles, based on their own prejudices. Just as a jazz purist might sneer at commercial or trad jazz, opprobrium is heaped upon acts such as Limp Bizkit and Korn once they achieve mainstream chart success.

The purpose of this book is not to draw up a definitive list of nu-metal bands, nor is it an attempt to establish rigid boundaries for the sort of rock that constitutes nu-metal. Indeed, many of the acts featured herein have publicly disassociated themselves from the genre. What you are holding is designed to be viewed as a wide-angle snapshot of new rock in the new millennium. What you make of it is your own business. It's only rock 'n' roll.

CROSSTOWN TRAFFIC
Fusion Rock

'It's a brand-new old thing.' – George Clinton

Heavy metal has never been a 'pure' medium. The term was coined by writer William Burroughs in his futuristic nightmare novel *Nova Express* (1964) – the Heavy Metal Kids being a group of junkies, who slow their metabolism until their spines are like 'frozen hydraulic jacks' – but was later employed by the legendary gonzoid critic Lester Bangs. An avid reader of Burroughs, Bangs used the phrase in his *Creem*, *Rolling Stone* and *Village Voice* articles to define the hyper-amplified, bass-heavy riffing of rock behemoths such as Blue Cheer. Elsewhere, Californian rockers Steppenwolf's 1968 biker anthem 'Born To Be Wild' famously included the phrase 'heavy metal thunder'. The song appeared on the soundtrack of the hippie road-movie *Easy Rider*, which intoduced the term into the hip-speak of the late sixties and early seventies.

'Heavy is for the white, what blues is for black people.' – Rob Halford

Improvisation and experimentation were long-established practices among jazz and, to a lesser extent, blues musicians, sometimes taking the music into entirely new areas. Traditional folk songs, spirituals, and work 'hollers' (as heard in the cotton fields and on prison chain-gangs) were all assimilated into the cultural mix – the structure and style of classical composers Liszt and Chopin influenced Black innovators like bluesman Robert Johnson and jump-jive band leader Cab Calloway. Successive generations of mainly Afro-American musicians were not afraid to mix and match influences. Blues and jazz mutated and cross-fertilised throughout the twentieth century, and the influence of the two forms is present within all modern musical styles. A prime example of this is the African/Mississippi Delta oral folk tradition from which the blues originates (the blues guitar following, or making reference to, the vocal). The lyrical content of the Southern slave song – telling of hardship, oppression and alienation – has distinct similarities to much modern rap.

As vocalist with Led Zeppelin, Robert Plant came to epitomise rock'n'roll.

The original Black Sabbath line up featuring, left to right: Terry 'Geezer' Butler, Tony Iommi, Ozzy Osbourne and Bill Ward.

In much the same way as rock 'n' roll was born out of the application of a strong backbeat to blues guitar, the origins of heavy metal lie in a re-application of hyper-amplified blues. The most obvious characteristic of the emerging style was that of excess. In terms of sheer volume, few could compete with bands such as Led Zeppelin, Deep Purple and Black Sabbath. Many commentators point to Zeppelin's eponymous 1969 debut as the recording that initially defined heavy metal. However, the album was simply representative of a development that had been taking place over a number of years. Jimi Hendrix had already become famous for his sonically-challenging fusion of blues and rock. His first two studio albums and bravura stage shows illustrated the way traditional blues structures could mutate into psychedelic rock. Other artists, notably Eric Clapton with Cream and Miles Davis, had explored similar avenues, respectively applying elements of rhythm 'n' blues and jazz to heavy rock and vice versa.

As more acts adopted a 'heavier' sound, the defining boundaries of the medium were expanded. Black Sabbath utilised satanic imagery, shrieking vocals and fast, tremolo-heavy guitar solos that would influence demon hordes of black/death metal performers.

In his third album, *Electric Ladyland*, Jimi Hendrix combined elements of

Jimi Hendrix's unique guitar genius opened up infinite rock fusion horizons.

heavy rock, blues and funk, setting a benchmark for the cross-cultural fusion of the next 30 years. It was this incorporation of funk with Hendrix's own 'blues-metal' that paved the way for artists such as George Clinton, Rick James and Jimmy Castor to mix and match diverse musical influences with the heavyweight funk of the 1970's.

The release of Funkadelic's self-titled debut in 1970 heralded an evolutionary leap in the fusion of rock and funk. Fronted by George Clinton, the band had been a 1950's/60's doo-wop outfit called the Parliaments before they were renamed Funkadelic following an ownership dispute over their title. Funkadelic appropriated aspects of heavy metal, blues, acid rock and jazz to frame the unique 'P-Funk Philos-o-phee' or 'P-Funk Theology'. (In the aftermath of psychedelia, this was a celebratory space-cadet view of music, the universe and everything – with tenets such as the 'Pinocchio Theory', warning against 'faking the funk [or your nose will grow]'.) Maverick talents such as Clinton, keyboard virtuoso Bernie Morrell and legendary bass genius William 'Bootsy' Collins set the Parliament-Funkadelic (or P-Funk) agenda. Drawing the distinction between his two most famous creations, Clinton reveals, 'Funkadelic was the guitar and rock side of the house and Parliament was for the singers and the horns.'

Clinton presided over a nebulous collective of singers and players that performed interchangeably for both bands, various side-projects (Bootsy's Rubber Band, the Brides of Funkenstein, and Collins' heavy metal outfit Zillatron) and diverse solo projects. Defined by Bootsy as 'the purest form of funk that you can get', Clinton's sprawling empire incorporated elements of science-fiction – 'the Mothership Connection', effectively a pimp-funk version of the *Close Encounters*-type myth – and a plethora of comic-book alter egos adopted by band personnel, exaggerating aspects of their creators' personalities within the schizoid, drug-fuelled universe of P-Funk. As Bootsy Collins said, 'Bootzilla is the monstrous character, he don't care what's happening, he's come to *let's take it to the stage*, he's into mashin' a mug. He's into heavy funk, heavy monster rock, he's loud, he's got the rhinestone rock star thang, the glasses, he's the glitter.'

The diversity of the P-Funk stable created an environment suited to cross-cultural experimentation. As Clinton recalls, 'Everybody in the group had different stuff that they wanted to do, an' they all got to play it, 'cause we developed a style that was basic in some ways, but really deep in others. I mean, we saw Jimi Hendrix playin' the blues, just puttin' a lot of effects on it. We saw James Brown vampin' and groovin' and takin' it to the bridge an' back. We saw all the Motown stuff that was just as sophisticated as it could possibly get. An' then there was Traffic and King Crimson an' groups that played jazz an' classical things in a rock setting. An' the singers were into, like, gospel while I was into tight vocals an' parts that I pushed to the max. [Guitarist] Tawl [Ross], he was into Iggy Pop and all that stuff that turned into punk. So I'd just always remember to throw *all* of that stuff into the mix to

George Clinton created a mythos of alter egos and superpowers amongst his P-Funk personnel. This illustration from his 1979 This Boot Is Made For Fonk-N *album depicts bassist Bootsy Collins in his 'Star Mon' incarnation.*

Funkadelic – Maggot Brain *(1971). Possibly the heaviest, funkiest album ever.*

confuse people.'

George Clinton's zeal for experimentation is regularly cited by such hip-hop innovators as Afrika Baambaata and Ice Cube as having a direct influence on their outlook and musical direction. Employing meandering lyrics that hark back to the oral roots of black music, while foreshadowing the development of rap, the P-Funk phenomenon has also left its mark on acts as diverse as the Red Hot Chili Peppers, Public Enemy and Limp Bizkit. Subsequent to a period of 'planned obsolescence' during the 1980s, Clinton has reconstituted his P-Funk All-stars and continues to stretch out in new directions. 'We got this whole new following, with the Lollapalooza shows we did and the *PCU* movie [a 1994 comedy about politically-correct college life, featuring music by Parliament]', testifies Clinton, 'and all the hip-hoppers sampling the music – we've got a whole new audience we didn't have before.'

'We developed a style that was basic in some ways, but really deep in others.' – George Clinton

While the likes of Clinton, Collins and slick funksters the Ohio Players readily brought rock toys to the funk playground, 1970s metal acts drew their influences from incestuously traditional areas. KISS recycled glam-rock mummery in a stadium-rock setting, while AC/DC, UFO and Thin Lizzy represented a back-to-basics approach. Playing shorter tunes than their grandiose prog-rock contemporaries, their lyrics were generally concerned with little more than fast living and hard drinking. As Judas Priest vocalist Rob Halford said of metal's blue-collar attitudes, 'Heavy is for the white, what blues is for black people.'

The New Wave of British Heavy Metal defined the template for heavy rock during the late seventies and early eighties. As established metal acts grew in popularity and performed in stadiums rather than clubs, bands such as Iron Maiden, Judas Priest and Saxon infused the traditional arena with new energy and enthusiasm. While they shared much common ground, the 'NWOBHM' groups also varied significantly: from the sledgehammer approach of Motorhead to the more mainstream pop purveyed by Def Leppard.

The NWOBHM was christened by *Sounds* journalist Geoff Barton – an avid advocate of the new bands, directly involved in compiling the 1980 *Metal for Muthas* anthology that did much to define the new territory. At the end of the day, however, it proved to be just another marketing pigeonhole. Like the nu-metal tag itself, the term could be applied to such a diverse range of bands that it verged on being meaningless.

Just as punk rock was a reaction to the dinosaur super-groups of the mid-1970's, the NWOBHM represented a return to raw denim-and-leather rock. Initially, at least, these London-based acts performed in smaller venues – while Rainbow or Whitesnake packed out the Rainbow or Hammersmith Odeon, Iron Maiden filled the Bridge House pub in Canning Town, in an atmosphere more akin to a punk gig than a Blue Oyster Cult concert. Many of these groups adopted a 'street' posture and it was this attitude, rather than any notable progression from what had gone on before, that defined this vague movement.

Inevitably, the groups that comprised the NWOBHM diversified in a similar manner to the original heavy metal outfits. Iron Maiden teamed up with former Samson vocalist Bruce Dickinson and evolved a more progressive sound; Judas Priest, who straddled the old and new waves of metal, embellished their chanting anthems with neo-classical guitar sections that would later influence death metal. Similarly, Venom have at various times been credited as the originators of death metal, speed metal, thrash metal, black metal and grindcore. The band themselves were more modest, describing their sound as 'dinosaur destroyer bass and vocals, chainsaw guitar and 125 inter-city express.' But however much the NWOBHM groups blurred the distinctions between heavy metal and punk, they never strayed outside the existing rock parameters.

Venom frontman Cronos. Thrash metal pioneers, the band influenced the likes of Slayer, Metallica and Slipknot.

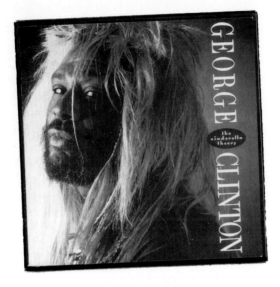

George Clinton's genius for experimentation and excess guided both Funkadelic and Parliament towards new, freaky frontiers.

While rock continued to regurgitate itself, the emergence of hip-hop in the mid-1970's continued the musical cross-pollination. Hip-hop originated among the block parties of the Bronx in New York City, where DJ's would rhyme over the beat of the record. This 'rapping' was reminiscent of the Jamaican tradition of dancehall 'toasting', whereby the MC would chant out complex, self-aggrandising or politically-charged lyrics over instrumental sections of popular reggae hits.

'In the future, there will be only one music . . . funk.' – Afrika Bambaataa

So well-established was this practice that most reggae 45's featured instrumental cuts of the main track on the b-side. Many of these 'version excursions' by producers such as Joe Gibbs and Lee 'Scratch' Perry incorporated unearthly and jarring sound effects. This experimentation gave rise to the 'dub' style later developed by technicians/performers like Scientist, Jah Shaka and Adrian Sherwood. Similarly, the growth in popularity of toasting, which was exported from Jamaica to the USA and Britain, gave rise to a whole generation of dancehall MC's including Yellowman, Eek-a-Mouse, Clint Eastwood and General Saint, and Toyan and Fathead.

Versed in the dancehall style, young Clive Campbell followed his mother from Trenchtown, Jamaica to the Bronx. Sharing his father's love of music – as well as much of the sound system he built – Campbell gave his first DJ performance in 1973 at a recreation centre on the ground floor of his housing block. Campbell would oversee the evolution of hip-hop in parks, parties, housing projects and local halls. Developing a technique of extending the instrumental breaks of songs by switching back and forth between two copies of the same record, he soon developed a reputation that enabled him to score regular bookings on the local club circuit, a nickname, 'DJ Kool Herc' (reference to Campbell's imposing stature), and

Parliament bassist Bootsy Collins – as part of George Clinton's funkier ensemble, Collins brought glam rock to funk.

a theme tune, 'Apache', by Jamaican disco group the Incredible Bongo Band. It was Herc's set that gave rise to the birth of the 'b-boys': local youths, priced out of Manhattan clubs, who saved their funkiest moves for the breaks – originating the 1980's phenomenon of break-dancing.

'Rap music developed out of local block parties in the black ghetto. These parties, often in housing projects, were associated with gangs who occupied their turf. To protect themselves and keep the peace at their parties, all well-known rap crews became affiliated with "security forces". Membership of security force crews like the Casanova Crew, the Nine Crew, and the Zulu Nation ranged from 600 to thousands. Most rappers were forced to find security from local "stick up kids". Security forces themselves were largely composed of hoodlums, although their energies were channelled into rap competition. Black gang warfare declined dramatically during this period (1978-81).'
Charles Henry, *Culture and African American Politics*

Kool Herc's contemporaries, pioneering MC's such as Coke La Rock and Lovebug Starski, borrowed from an eclectic range of pre-recorded material to provide the breaks, beats and scratching that became synonymous with the music. While relying heavily on the technology of the day, the main elements of hip-hop, rapping, sampling and scratching all had their roots in antiquity. Much rap consisted of personal anecdotes, harking back to the storytelling tradition associated with black music's folkloric origins. Similarly, the technique of drawing the needle back across a record to produce a scratched rhythm was directly related to the use of a brushed snare drum in jazz, or the rattles and gourds found in the most primitive forms of music.

Born of urban deprivation, it was hardly surprising that rap's political devel-

Unlike 'Rapper's Delight', seminal Sugar Hill release 'The Message' told the real story of hip-hop street-life.

opment mirrored its musical progress. During the late 1960's, street poets like Gil Scott-Heron and the Last Poets continued a tradition of politicised rapping that originated with the African 'griots', or slave-chanters, and extended through the be-bop poets and radio DJ's of the previous decade. The Last Poets' self-titled debut album, along with subsequent early seventies releases *Chastisements* and *This Is Madness,* have become classics of Afro-American consciousness. Indeed, it was a Last Poet, Lightning Rod, who recorded the mid-seventies proto-rap 'Hustler's Convention', which became a mainstay of early hip-hop DJ's. Using the spoken word over a minimal backing, often consisting entirely of rhythm, these performers foreshadowed the rap aesthetic in content as well as style – acts such as Public Enemy and Rage Against the Machine ultimately extending this tradition into the modern era.

The first global rap hit, the Sugarhill Gang's 'Rappers Delight' (1979), relied heavily upon the bassline from elegant soulsters Chic's 'Good Times' with the trio simply rapping over the rhythm. The lengthy rap's first four onomatopoeic lines rapidly became the 'awopbopaloobopabopbamboom!' of the b-boy generation: 'I said a hip-hop, the hippy, the hippy / to the hip, hip-hop, you don't stop / the rockit to the bang bang boogie, say up jumped the boogie / to the rhythm of the boogie, the beat.' Climbing to fourth spot on the *Billboard* R&B chart, the song immediately overshadowed the release, some months earlier, of the Fatback Band's 'King Tim III (Personality Jock)', a standard piece of seventies disco that featured a brief rap, section credited as the first rap song committed to vinyl.

The Sugarhill Gang were devised as a house rap act by Sugarhill records supremo Sylvia Robinson. A former R&B vocalist, Robinson was notable for having recorded the sultry 1973 hit 'Pillow Talk', with her husband Joe. Having been impressed by the nascent Harlem rap scene, Robinson recruited former bouncer Hank Jackson, whose sole involvement with music had been as manager of Bronx rap crew the Cold Crush Brothers. Enlisting Cold Crush rapper Grandmaster Caz, Jackson – armed only with Caz's book of rhymes – recorded the track along with two other unknown rappers, Michael Wright and Guy O'Brien.

'Rap music developed out of local block parties in the black ghetto.' – Charles Henry

Their debut single was an international success, yet the Sugarhill Gang were not actually representative of the hip-hop scene. Manufactured by Robinson, the trio were backed by a studio band rather than laying down the vocals over pre-recorded vinyl. However, Sugarhill Records built upon the success of 'Rapper's Delight' with a string of soul, funk and rap hits throughout the early 1980's. In addition to the Sugarhill Gang, the Robinsons recruited rap acts such as the Funky Four + One, the Treacherous Three and the South Carolina-based female trio Sequence. However, with the release of their 1982 single 'The Message', Grandmaster Flash and the Furious Five became Sugarhill's most successful act. The record was a follow-up to the previous year's 'The Adventures of Grandmaster Flash on the Wheels of Steel', which introduced scratching and cutting – the DJ techniques of using record decks like a musical instrument, switching back and forth between dual or multiple decks with a cross-fader – to a mass audience. Flash (real name Joseph Saddler) was an accomplished DJ credited with developing the 'clock method' of scratching (whereby a DJ would establish the correct point to drop the needle, by mapping out a disc in parallel to the times on a clock face). 'Wheels of Steel' lifted cuts from Queen's 'Another One Bites the Dust', Blondie's 'Rapture' (featuring a rapped vocal by Deborah Harry and name-checks for DJ's Flash and Herc) and the by-now ubiquitous 'Good Times'. By committing these techniques to record, 'Wheels of Steel' represented a far more accurate portrayal of hip-hop's block-party origins than 'Rapper's Delight', establishing a trend followed by all subsequent hip-hop DJ's. 'The Message' (1982) featured no cuts and little sampling, evoking instead the realities of the street through its politicised rap – its narrator complaining of 'Broken glass everywhere/people pissing on the sidewalk 'cos they just don't care.' The grim scenario climaxes with a young wanna-be 'gangsta' hanging himself in his prison cell, and the narrator warning, 'Don't push me/'cos I'm close to the edge.' Regardless of Sugarhill's reservations about the song's content, the record went platinum and won a *Rolling Stone* 'Single of the Year' award.

As leader of the notorious Black Spades street gang, Afrika Bambaataa (born Kevin Donovan) was responsible for organising security at Herc's block-party throw-downs. Ever astute, Bambaataaa was not slow in realising the possibilities of hip-hop: 'I liked what he was playing, it sounded funky, and I had all that shit at home – all those records he was playing – so I said, once I come out and get my system, I'm gonna start playing that too.' Bambaataa was known as an atypical gang lead-er, fiercely hostile to drugs and quick to promote self-development among his peers. As the mid-1970's New York street-gang culture dissolved amidst violence, arrests and drug fatalities, 'Bam', as he became widely known, saw the block-party scene as an opportunity for some personal self-development.

'Hip-hop itself is colourless, it's taken from all different types of music that make the beat and that funk, it's what you put on top as your lyrics that make it for black people, white people or uni-versal.' – Afrika Bambaataa

In 1979, Tom Silverman, the one-man workforce behind the magazine *Disco News,* became intrigued by word of DJ sessions fronted by Bambaataa and his Zulu Nation and resolved to check out the action. The club that he visited was located in the South Bronx, in an upstairs room on White Plains Road. 'Bambaataa was DJ-ing,' Silverman recalls, 'but a lot of the time he was just picking the records and giv-ing them to Jazzy Jay or Red Alert, who were the two DJ's that he had at the time. They would put the records on . . . I remember Whiz Kid was playing bass on stage once the music was going and then somebody else was up there rapping. That was the first time I heard people actually rapping to these breakbeats. Most of the time it was just beats going on and on and there was no DJ.' Silverman made Bambaataa an on-the-spot offer: 'I went right up there and I got with him afterwards.'

Silverman took his tentative first steps into record production by releasing a disco single through a small underground record label. Undaunted by the absence of any backing, he formed his own independent label which he modestly chris-tened Tommy Boy. The first release on the new label was a twelve-inch disco plate, 'Havin' Fun'. Recorded by an obscure group named Cotton Candy, the single incorporated a brief rap from Bam and his MC's, the Soul Sonic Force (Mr Biggs,

Afrika Bambaataa and the Soul Sonic Force: responsible for the classic track 'Planet Rock' which fused hip-hop and electro in ground-breaking style.

Pow Wow and G.L.O.B.E.). Soon after, the quartet recorded a demo tape for Silverman, entitled *In the Red*, which he played to an associate – a former Boston DJ turned aspiring producer named Arthur Baker. Galvanised by the streetbeat of Bam and the Force, Baker collaborated with Silverman and the band on a reworking of Gwen McRae's disco hit, 'Funky Sensation'. Retitled 'Jazzy Sensation' and backed with a remix produced by leading New York DJ Shep Pettibone, the twelve-inch sold out of its original pressing and took Tommy Boy Records out of the red.

Arthur Baker describes himself as 'a DJ-producer who got into remixing'. In much the same manner as the synergy between Rick Rubin and Russell Simmons would be vital to the development of Run DMC, the Beastie Boys and rap in general, so Baker's relationship with Silverman was key to the movement of early-eighties rap away from the established rhythm-and-rhyme format epitomised by Kurtis Blow (the pioneering rapper behind the 1979 hit 'Christmas Rappin'') and Grandmaster Flash. Explaining the necessity of this progression, Afrika Bambaataa remembers, 'I was looking at all the other rap records. Everyone was talking the same thing, talking about theyself, talking about how bad he is, how many girls he could get. I said, "We need something different."' Similarly, Baker applied his remixing skills to taking hip-hop – which he sees as 'the most technical and least technical kind of music' – forward. As the producer behind 'Put the Needle to the Record', released under the name Criminal Element Orchestra, Baker (along with hip-hop montagists Double D and Steinski) was responsible for the cut 'n' paste production technique that was the precursor of modern digital sampling.

Visually, Bambaataa and the Soul Sonic Force screamed for attention. Early pictures of the band show them looking for all the world like a black punk band, complete with bleached hairstyles, leather and studs. Taking inspiration from George Clinton, Bambaataa developed the quartet's image along similar comic-

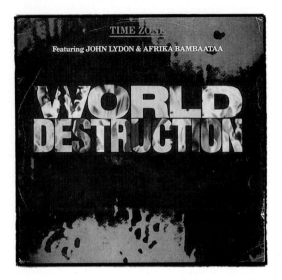

Afrika Bambaataa and punk icon John Lydon joined forces on the pivotal record 'World Destruction'.

book lines to those affected by the P-Funk crew. This, along with Bam's vocoder-enhanced rapping, and the use of ersatz future technology in early promotional videos, gave the Force a science-fiction image not dissimilar from the funk-o-nauts of Clinton's Mothership. Indeed, the extended video for 'Planet Rock' features an introductory sequence where Bambaataa, shot in close-up with banks of flashing lights reflecting across his shades, announces (through a vocoder), 'In the future, there will be only one music . . . funk.'

'"Planet Rock" – the style and the music, is the most sampled record in the history of hip-hop and the most copied sound in the world.' - Monica Lynch

It was this, Bambaataa's second release in 1982, which redefined the boundaries of hip-hop. 'Planet Rock' was inspired by Bambaataa's admiration for German proto-industrialists Kraftwerk and featured a fusion of their 'Trans Europe Express' with Bam's authoritative vocal delivery. Keyboard player John Robie was recruited to provide the record's European electro element. 'I hung out with him a bit and this guy was amazing on the synthesizer,' recalls Bam. 'So I said "Can you play stuff like Kraftwerk?" He said "I'll tear that shit up." He would play stuff like that and I was like "Whoa, this guy is BAD." I had been with Arthur [Baker] who did "Jazzy Sensation" with us and I told him he had to meet this guy. So that's when the Soul Sonic Force got together with the electro-funk sound. It all just took off from there.'

The resultant combination of powerful street poetry and clinical technology proved irresistible, and 'Planet Rock' (often cited as the starting point for electro-rap) was an immediate success. Tommy Boy's Monica Lynch recalls, 'It was amazing to walk around Manhattan and that record was coming out of every window, every car. That was really the record that put us on the map.' The track was the only certified gold twelve-inch single of 1982 and still remains hugely influential. As Bambaataa explains, '"Planet Rock" – the style and the music, is the most sampled record in the history of hip-hop and the most copied sound in the world. I come down to New Zealand and they're all "Planet Rock" crazy. Then they got all the Miami Bass, which is electro-funk crazy. Latin hip-hop, when they were doing the freestyle, they were "Planet Rock" crazy. In England you hear the "Planet Rock" grooves in many things. Even in the jungle beats, you slow it down and you hear it. It's just amazing how that record has just kept on going, going, going.' As Silverman concurs, 'That ended up on a billion records afterwards.'

Credited as the godfather of hip-hop, Bambaataa defines it holistically as 'the whole culture . . . There's the rap, which is a form of hip-hop culture. It could be breakdancing, freestyle dancing or whatever type of dancing that's happening now in the Black, Hispanic and White communities. That is hip-hop, meaning the whole culture.' In support of this aesthetic of musical fusion, he reveals, 'You can take music from any type of field like soul, funk, heavy metal, jazz, calypso and reggae. As long as it's funky and has that heavy beat and groove. You can take any part of it to make hip-hop.'

Throughout the decade, Bambaataa continued to draw upon diverse influences. Having had a follow-up hit with 'Looking for the Perfect Beat', a similar slice of Baker-produced proto-electro, he established a second persona: Shango, performing a harder-edged form of funk, which, both visually and musically, owed much to the influence of George Clinton. In 1984 he embarked on the first of a series of collaborative projects, 'Unity', recorded with the resurgent James Brown. The song was not only an espousal of Bambaataa's progressive ideals of self-improvement, peace, unity and musical community, but also a homage to the godfather of funk. Following the release of a single with Melle

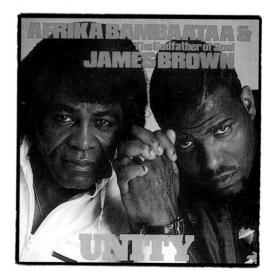

James Brown and Afrika Bambaataa teamed up for the 1985 hit "Unity".

Afrika Bambaataa and the Soul Sonic Force: Renegades of Funk *(1983). Hip-hop utilised influences from all aspects of popular culture. In this instance, comic books.*

Mel (who was enjoying greater success than his former mentor Grandmaster Flash), 'Who Do You Think You're Funkin' With?', Bambaataa again broke new ground by inviting punk to the hip-hop party in the form of ex-Pistol John Lydon. 'World Destruction' was released under the collective name Time Zone in 1985, and featured Bambaataa and Lydon vocalising a portentous, apocalyptic lyric: 'Nostradamus predicts the coming of the Antichrist/Hey, look out, the third world nations are on the rise!' While not making a huge impact upon the charts, the recording introduced Bambaataa, and rap music in general, to a new, white audience. The collaboration between the leader of the Zulu Nation (now grown from being a group of security enforcers to encompass all of Bam's following) and the poster-child of punk may have seemed incongruous, but Bam identified an historical context: 'It was the punk rockers and new wavers that were the first of all white people to accept this music. They were bringing me down to the punk rock clubs to mix. You used to see punk rockers come up to jam at the hardcore Black and Hispanic neighbourhoods.'

Bambaataa's commitment to experimentation was further demonstrated on his album release that year, *Beware the Funk Is Everywhere*, which featured versions of 'Kick out the Jams' (originally recorded by Detroit proto-punks the MC5) and John Carpenter's atmospheric theme from the action movie *Assault on Precinct 13*. As he explains, 'I'm the Renegade of Funk, I'll do what I want to do. That's why I've made house, techno, rock, funk, reggae and soca.' By combining various musical genres in an original way, the pioneering rappers and DJ's laid the groundwork for later crossover artists.

The Clash: Paul Simonon, Nicky 'Topper' Headon, Joe Strummer, Mick Jones.

PUNKY REGGAE PARTY
The Clash and American Hardcore

'Each generation needs a soundtrack and the
Clash provided mine . . .' – Don Letts, DJ/filmmaker

By the early 1980's, the British punk scene was undergoing its noisy, drawn-out death throes. The class of '76 had either split up (the Sex Pistols, the Slits, X-Ray Spex), changed direction or, as with peripheral acts like the Jam and the Stranglers, been absorbed by the mainstream.

By far the most important and influential of the original punk bands were the Clash. Since the release of their self-titled debut in 1977, the quartet of Joe Strummer, Mick Jones, Paul Simonon and Topper Headon had stood out from the three-chord horde by virtue of the political *savoir-faire* of their lyrics and the assimilation of reggae into their urban-guerrilla sound. *The Clash* featured a reworking of the Junior Murvin/Lee Perry reggae classic 'Police and Thieves', which confirmed reggae as every punk rocker's second favourite musical style. An association with Rastafarian filmmaker Don Letts widened the band's sphere of musical influences beyond the constraints of rock. For his part, Letts contributed to the cross pollination of musical styles by becoming the resident DJ at the Roxy Club, which was the epicentre of the London punk scene during 1976-77. As DJ, Letts dished up generous helpings of dub and roots for the nightly punk throng. Recalling this period, Letts explains, 'Punk was so new [that] none of the bands had actually released any records yet. So I played what I was into – reggae, especially dub.' 2002 saw the release of a compilation album, *Dread Meets Punk Rockers Uptown*, which features many of the tracks Letts played at the Roxy and includes dub legends such as King Tubby and Big Youth.

The Clash's next two albums, *Give 'Em Enough Rope* (1978) and *London Calling* (1979), furthered the ethos of fusion, with tracks such as the dub-driven 'Guns of Brixton' borrowing from the reggae canon – the track itself later heavily sampled by Norman Cook on his Beats International smash 'Dub Be Good to Me'. While not limiting their diversification strictly to reggae (the band incorporated elements of jazz, swing, traditional rock 'n' roll and Latin American rhythms), single releases such as 'White Man in Hammersmith Palais' and 'Bank Robber' (co-written and recorded with dancehall superstar Mikey Dread) cemented the band's relationship with Jamaican music.

The dawn of the 1980's saw the Clash disillusioned with Margaret Thatcher's conservative government. Keen to establish themselves in America, the band embarked on a series of Stateside tours which gained them a solid following. The Clash were quick to adopt elements of the host culture, assimilating elements of rap into the 1981 hit 'The Magnificent Seven' that received airplay from rap-orientated radio stations like New York's EBLS-FM. When the group touched down for a seventeen-night stint at Bond's International Casino in Times Square, they handed the support slot to Grandmaster Flash and the Treacherous Three. Sadly, American punks did not share the varied tastes of their British counterparts, and the rappers were greeted with a hail of missiles and abuse.

The pressures of constant touring caused the Clash to separate during 1983. Strummer and Simonon recorded a final album, *Cut the Crap,* with a stand-in line-

The Clash brought multi-racial politics to punk rock. The backdrop behind the band depicts an image from the riot at the 1976 Notting Hill Carnival.

Slits vocalist Ari Up. The Slits infused their mix of punk and reggae with a sense of chaos.

up before pronouncing the group dead. The band's musical driving force, guitarist Mick Jones, continued to experiment with the fusion of hip-hop and rap. Forming Big Audio Dynamite with Don Letts, he produced two albums that grafted rap, sampling and beat boxes to a rock template. Jones and Strummer reunited briefly for a benefit gig in November 2002, leading to speculation that the band might reform. Joe Strummer's death in December 2002 came as a huge shock, putting a tragic full-stop on the Clash legend.

Like the Clash, the Slits were not slow in splicing dub-driven rhythms to rock guitars. Originally an all female group, the band had previously toured with the Clash and the Sex Pistols. Capriciously brilliant, yet always teetering on the verge of chaos, their early performances were the raucous epitome of '77 punk. By 1979, the Slits had re-worked their entire 'Slitrock' repertoire to incorporate the reggae rhythms provided by bassist Tessa Pollitt and the future Siouxsie and the Banshees drummer, Budgie; a dub backing which gave the group a unique sound. The band's first album *Cut* (produced by reggae heavyweight Dennis Bovell) was released in 1979 to unrestrained acclaim and reasonable sales. Whilst they toured extensively between 1976 and 1981, the band managed only one further album before scattering to distant corners of the globe. 1981's *Return of the Giant Slits* saw the band venture deeper into dubwise territory and marked their only album release for new label CBS.

During this period ex-Pistol John Lydon, a long-time reggae fan, was engaged to act as the Jamaican-based talent scout for Virgin Records' Front Line subsidiary. Lydon subsequently returned to the UK to form Public Image Ltd, and the impact of his sojourn in the home of reggae can be heard throughout P.I.L.'s second album, *Metal Box*. Recorded on three twelve-inch 45 rpm discs to enhance the bass tones, the rhythms provided by drummer Martin Atkins and bassist Jah Wobble owe much to the dub stylings of Joe Gibbs and King Tubby. Wobble, a former London Underground ticket collector from East London, later went on to record his own 'dub-heavy' album, *Betrayal,* which was largely based around master tapes 'appropriated' from Public Image sessions.

'The Gang of Four know how to swing, I stole a lot from them.' – Michael Stipe (REM)

With the emphasis on creative experimentation that characterised the initial wave of UK punk bands, other musical elements were brought to bear on the genre. As the seventies drew to a close, bands such as Leeds-based quartet the Gang of Four and Bristol's the Pop Group assimilated funk within their anarchic musical frameworks. Taking their political cues from the Clash and their rhythms from the R 'n' B chart, the Gang of Four's breakthrough album *Entertainment* was indicative of the diverse frontiers explored by the first post-punk generation. In particular Andy Gill's intermittent guitar breaks eerily foreshadow the techniques later used by Rage Against the machine's Tom Morello to approximate scratching effects. The impact of the Gang of Four was far-reaching, with the likes of Red Hot Chili Peppers' bassist Flea citing them as an influence.

Despite this emphasis on diversity and cross-cultural fusion, punk did not particularly appeal to the black UK audience. Black punk rockers were few and far between and it is true to say that punk's appreciation of reggae was rarely reciprocated by their dreadlocked brethren. However, a welcome exception to this rule arrived in the shape of the Basement 5. Decked out in white boiler suits and ski goggles, the quartet served up a punky blend of techno-reggae that was easily ten years ahead of its time. Don Letts had originally been approached to serve as the band's frontman but, after showing some initial enthusiasm, dropped out and was replaced by the noted photographer Dennis Morris. Like the Slits, the Basement 5 were signed by Island Records, releasing two singles ('Silicon Chip', 'Last White Xmas') and an album (*1965-80*) before dropping from sight in 1981. While the Clash were exploring the USA, the punk scene that the band was once an integral part of was disintegrating. The newer, more visceral acts tended to be either politicised proto-thrash (Discharge, Conflict) or anarchist collectives such as Crass. There

The Basement 5's only album release, 1965-80, fused punk and reggae in groundbreaking style.

was little sign of any musical innovation, and the imaginative fashions worn by the original punks had long given way to a uniform of spiky hair, leather jacket, studs and boots. The emergence of the largely right-wing 'Oi' bands championed by *Sounds'* Garry Bushell, such as the 4-Skins and the Business, had delivered a good helping of mindless violence courtesy of the skinhead revival. The unpleasant right-wing posturing of these bands, along with events following a Business gig in 1981 that precipitated the Southall riot, served to trammel that particular branch of punk toward a monocultural cul de sac. By the time Crass dissolved in 1984, there was no British punk rock and very few punks.

'I think the only reason why major labels picked up on grunge and punk to begin with was to avoid a whole generation of suburban white kids getting their political knowledge from angry black rappers.'
Jello Biafra

Things were more vibrant in America, where the scene that bred groups such as the Dead Kennedys, Black Flag (fronted by former ice-cream parlour manager Henry Rollins) and Husker Du had taken a little longer to develop. This was no bad thing, as the spectrum of what became known as US 'hardcore' was far broader than in the UK. The San Francisco-based Dead Kennedys, led by charismatic political activist Jello Biafra, were defined both by their opposition to the hard right – epitomised by the 'moral majority' and TV evangelists such as Jerry Falwell – and the 'nazi hippies' of West Coast liberalism. The name 'Dead Kennedys' itself was formulated to provoke simultaneous disgust in conservative and liberal America, in much the same way Marilyn Manson later hit upon a nomenclature the older generation would find almost universally offensive. Musically, the band had a standard 'melodic punk' sound, redolent of the high-speed blitzkrieg pop of the Ramones and the Buzzcocks, drifting into thrash for numbers such as 'Nazi Punks Fuck Off'

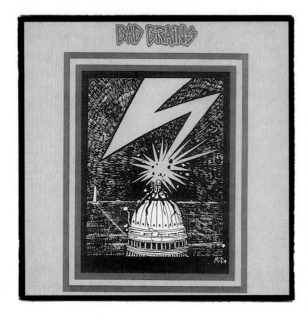

The (cd re-issue) cover image of the eponymous, cassette-only, debut album from Washington DC hardcore legends Bad Brains.

or crossing over into the dark pop layering of 'Moon Over Marin' on the album *Plastic Surgery Disasters*. Their confrontational choice of subject matter was epitomised by four consecutive singles: 'California Uber Alles', 'Holiday in Cambodia', 'Kill the Poor' and 'Too Drunk to Fuck'. Born out of the punk aesthetic, Biafra's cynical view of corporate America would later inspire polemical bands like Rage Against the Machine and Amen.

But there was much more to the US hardcore scene than a slew of bands aping the Dead Kennedys' sound and image. While the Kennedys ploughed a relentless musical furrow, elements of jazz, psychedelia and heavy metal were spliced into punk by bands such as the Minutemen, the Butthole Surfers and the Circle Jerks. Refuting criticism that his band were effectively a heavy metal outfit, Black Flag guitarist Greg Ginn explained, 'It's really hard to say we are this or that, because there's all kinds of influences musically and otherwise with our band. We listen to such diverse stuff.'

Musically, many hardcore bands favoured a more melodic approach to punk, closer to the Buzzcocks than the Sex Pistols – although their songs' breathless velocity meant they frequently lasted less than one minute. Groups such as the Descendents (an East Coast group who combined a melodic punk sound with goofy teen-angst lyricism) and Bad Religion, who remain active to this day, are the direct antecedents of modern pop-punk acts such as Green Day, Blink 182 and Sum 41.

The US hardcore scene of the day epitomised the punk DIY aesthetic, quickly spawning a network of independent labels such as Alternative Tentacles and SST to distribute the rapidly diversifying bands. Of these, Bad Brains were possibly the most innovative, fusing elements of reggae, punk and heavy metal in an accomplished manner that would influence Rage Against the Machine, Dub War and Body Count. Characterised on their debut single, 'Pay to Cum', by a blisteringly heavy guitar sound combined with vocals delivered at breakneck speed by Paul Hudson (HR) Bad Brains were the first Rastafarian hardcore outfit. 'Reggae music energises!' proclaimed bassist Darryl Jennifer, also acknowledging, 'There were bands before us. The Clash . . . were sort of reggae rock.' In a 1982 interview with underground hardcore-zine *Ripper*, vocalist HR described his own influences as Jah (the Rastafarian God), Bob Marley, Stevie Wonder and the Dickies (late-seventies punky popsters, remembered for covering the *Banana Splits* theme at lunatic velocity). Describing the Dickies' high-octane sound, Hudson recalls, 'When I first heard their music I said, "Gee it's so fast, this is really bad!" That's what made me really start liking fast rock 'n' roll, which eventually led into hardcore.'

'Punk was so new [that] none of the bands had actually released any records yet. So I played what I was into – reggae, especially dub.' – Don Letts

The band released their eponymous debut album on the ROIR label in 1982. Despite the limitations of a cassette-only format, Bad Brains received grass-roots acclaim on both sides of the Atlantic. Musically, the album mirrored the group's live set with several well-crafted roots reggae excursions interspersing their characteristically relentless hardcore assault. This success was followed by two twelve-inch EP's, both consisting of material from the cassette which, despite the format, also hit the UK Independent charts in 1983. Later that year, Bad Brains' first album proper, *Rock for Light*, achieved a similar degree of success.

Given the diversity of Bad Brains sound, it's ironic that this same pluralism ultimately led to their demise, with HR and drummer Earl Hudson leaving to produce a more traditional form of roots reggae in 1986. The band has periodically reformed, with both original and new personnel, but without the same momentum that propelled them during the early eighties.

Walk this way: original kings of rap-rock Run DMC, in changing formation. Top: Joseph Simmons, Darryl McDaniels, Jason Mizell; centre: Joseph, Jason, Darryl; bottom: rewind, in reverse order.

KINGS OF ROCK
Run DMC

'We broke that . . . we broke the mould by getting rap on MTV.' – Darryl McDaniels, Run DMC

When Steven Tyler of Aerosmith smashed through the wall of the recording-studio set in the video for 'Walk this Way', he was breaking down the barriers between rock and black music that had been creaking ever since Hendrix first fused funk and acid rock. Along with Run DMC and Def Jam supremos Russell Simmons and Rick Rubin, he would define a sound that made metal simultaneously hip and commercial for the first time. 'Walk this Way' is also the point at which hip-hop finally leapt the boundaries of race and colour.

Originally from the solidly middle-class neighbourhood of Hollis in Queens, New York, Run DMC had been chipping away at American mainstream consciousness since 1984, when their third single, 'Rock Box', received coverage on MTV. This represented a major breakthrough, given the channel's widely publicised fear and loathing of black music. Undoubtedly, it was the upfront incorporation of session guitarist Eddie Martinez's rock riffs into their music, which opened the minds of the MTV schedulers enough to give them some exposure.

'We came dressed as is, and that's what made the fans relate to us . . .' – Darryl McDaniels

The band – initially Run (Joseph Simmons) and DMC (Darryl McDaniels), later joined by a DJ, JamMaster Jay (Jason Mizell) – saw the opportunities afforded by an expanded audience and developed the rock element of their sound. The trio were astutely managed by Run's brother Russell, a former sociology student who co-founded Def Jam Records with Rick Rubin and went on to preside over Rush Communications – a small label that became a more financially successful corporation than Motown. Subsequent to their first two singles, 'It's Like That' and 'Hard Times', the band accepted a greater degree of creative input from Rubin, an old-school rocker with a rap sensibility. Describing his personal motivation for the shotgun marriage of rap and rock, Rubin reveals, 'I was going to NYU [New York University] and I was into rap music at the time, but there weren't a lot of rap records coming out; and the rap records that were coming out weren't representative of what the rap scene really was. I used to go to the rap clubs in New York – I'd be the only white guy there – and they'd be playing rock 'n' roll records with guys rapping over them. "Walk this Way" was an original record that every rap DJ would have and use. Billy Squire's "Big Beat" was another one. And the rap records that were coming out at the time were like Sugarhill Records, which were essentially disco records with people rapping over them. Kids who liked rap bought them because there weren't any records representative of their rap scene. So, I saw this void and started making those records, just because I was a fan and wanted them to exist.'

Run DMC released their self-titled debut album in May 1984 and quickly followed this with a second, *King of Rock*, early the next year. The album's title track, while effectively a simple re-working of 'Rock Box', proved a massive success as a single. 'King of Rock' gained the trio mainstream recognition on both sides of the Atlantic and established the aural template for the initial fusion of rock and rap.

> *'We used to rap over rock records before we got a chance to make our own records because we had to find records with beats. And rock records, James Brown records, they always had a break in them where the drums would just play, and maybe a bassline would play with the drum, or maybe a rock guitar would play with the drum, 'cause we couldn't rap over the vocals. So rock, not just for Run DMC, but for every rapper before us, was a big part of our repertoire.'* Darryl McDaniels

The only rap act to perform at 1985's Live Aid concerts, Run DMC began 1986 with top billing in the film *Krush Groove* – produced as a showcase for Def Jam, and featuring stable mates LL Cool J, Kurtis Blow and the Fat Boys. Built around a superficial light romantic plot, the film, modelled loosely on the genesis of Def Jam itself, centred on the trials of a struggling rap band – Run DMC. Although little more than a black version of the Ramones' *Rock 'n' Roll High School*, the film achieved its goal of exposing rap to a wider audience. It also introduced the Beastie Boys as fully-fledged members of the Def Jam stable, following their transition from punk to rap crossover.

As the film was receiving negative publicity on account of violence in US theatres (a phenomenon that did no commercial damage to Bill Haley or the Sex Pistols, when trouble flared during screenings of *Rock around the Clock* or *The Great Rock 'n' Roll Swindle),* Run DMC released their three million-selling *Raising Hell*

Darryl and Joseph pictured for the cover of their 1984 debut album.

album. Alongside the rap/rock fusion, the record featured more traditional raps such as 'My Adidas' and 'You Be Illin''. 'My Adidas' referred to a penchant shared by both the band and breakdancing hip-hoppers for the products of the German sportswear company. For Adidas tracksuits – along with black pork-pie hats, wide-framed Cazal sunglasses and leather box jackets – gave the group a street-level image that made them the first rap crew to score a major sponsorship deal with a clothing manufacturer, and undoubtedly set a precedent for Adidas' deal with Korn some years later. Although dismissed as a cynical marketing ploy, McDaniels insists the relationship authentically represented the trio's fashion sense: 'We came dressed as is, and that's what made the fans relate to us more than any other rap band because when they looked up on stage . . . it was like looking in a mirror.'

Raising Hell encompassed the entire spectrum of Run DMC's sound, from the complex rap-interplay of tracks like 'Perfection' and 'Peter Piper' to the highly MTV-friendly 'It's Tricky' (a cover of Toni Basil's lightweight pop hit 'Micky'). However, it was the combination of rap gymnastics and thunderous metal riffs that

Run DMC's third album, Raising Hell,
featured their re-working of Aerosmith's 'Walk This Way'.

established the band's reputation as a pioneering fusion act. While the new album's title track, 'Raising Hell', was well received, it was the re-working of Aerosmith's 'Walk This Way' that simultaneously won the band an international audience and revived interest in the Boston rockers. Describing the impact of the promotional video, MTV editorial director Michael Shore explains, 'This was the birth of the rap/rock movement that has now brought us Kid Rock and Limp Bizkit. Aerosmith being in the same space as Run DMC and seeming to enjoy it, both in the studio and on the stage, said a lot to people. It was like the seal of approval. And it meant it was easier for MTV to play, because Aerosmith was involved. MTV wasn't playing rap music then at all – it was only in 1983 with Michael Jackson that MTV started playing black music . . . But this video broke the bar for rap music. It played a huge role in getting rap accepted in the suburbs by white people.'

Rick Rubin, however, saw the historic musical fusion as a natural development: 'It didn't seem, for me, as unusual as it did for other people. I grew up with rap music and with rock music, and they always felt like different versions of the same thing to me . . . if you listen to "Walk This Way" by Aerosmith, it really is not that different from rap.'

'I used to go to the rap clubs in New York – I'd be the only white guy there – and they'd be playing rock'n'roll records with guys rapping over them.' – Rick Rubin

Raising Hell was the high point of Run DMC's career. Subsequent releases sold steadily (the fourth album, *Tougher than Leather*, being the last to go platinum) but were viewed as a disappointment when compared with the massive success enjoyed by the group between 1984-87. But the rock/rap template established by the group was inherited by Rush Productions stable-mates such as LL Cool J and the Beastie Boys. Indeed, Run and Darryl wrote the Beasties' hit 'Slow and Low', for which they were credited for 'special knowledge' on the *Licensed to Ill* album. The dynamic shouted raps of Run and Darryl had been similarly appropriated and developed by the new generation of rap acts, particularly Def Jam's own urban guerrillas Public Enemy. Undeterred by their downturn in fortunes, the band shifted their emphasis to the live performances that McDaniels regarded as the key to their longevity: 'Most hip-hop bands have got a life span of either one to three years . . . and that's it. That's why in Run DMC we don't focus on the record making, we focus on how many shows are we going to do this month . . . the only reason we lasted so long is because we're doing what was done before hip-hop records were made.'

Despite this, Run DMC left a legacy that laid the groundwork for nu-metal, and came full circle when acts such as Kid Rock and the former House of Pain rapper Everlast guested on the trio's most recent release, *Crown Royal*.

The seemingly motiveless murder of Jay (Jason Mizell) in October 2002 makes for a tragic postscript to Run DMC's career. Jay was shot once in the head at close range with a .40 calibre automatic whilst playing video games in the lounge of his Queens recording studio. Given Run DMC's ethos of peace and positivity, it's particularly poignant that their DJ should meet his end in such a violent manner. Public Enemy front man Chuck D paid tribute to his friend: 'I'm very, very deeply saddened, as well as angered, over the loss of a man who was both a hero and a good friend of mine. We were allies and friends, travelled the world together, shared our thoughts and good times, and watched each other's children grow up.' In the the immediate aftermath of Jay's murder, Run and Daryl announced they would not continue without their turntablist.

The Beastie Boys: Ad Rock (centre) sports the chain that damaged a thousand camper vans.

LOUDER THAN A B
Def Jam

'When you think about it, hardcore and hip-hop aren't that different. The attitude is the same.' – Adam Horowitz, the Beastie Boys

Rick Rubin was still a student at NYU when he first met Russell Simmons, brother of Run DMC's Joseph. Simmons was also studying (at New York City College) and had already established himself as a promoter of rap parties and events. Both Simmons and Rubin had already released records, but were frustrated with the lack of revenue filtering down through the independent label structure. As Rubin explains, 'I never got paid, and I learned how the independent record business works; I still haven't been paid to this date. And I met Russell Simmons, who had made about twenty hit records that sold a lot, and he was broke. He never got paid either. So I said, "This is dumb. They're not really doing much for us, and they're not paying us, so let's do it ourselves. At least we can make sure we get paid and our artists get paid."' As a duo they established Def Jam ('the Definitive Jam'), the label that was to become the pre-eminent arena for the rock and rap fusion.

Simmons handled the promotional aspects of the business through his company Rush Management, leaving Rubin largely free to concentrate on production. Simmons and Rubin not only personified the cross-cultural ethos of combining white and black music, but provided a bridge between their streetwise stable of performers and the commercial mainstream of the industry.

The first significant release from the label was teenage rapper LL Cool J's debut, 'I Need a Beat'. Cool J (aka James Todd Smith) had been brought up in Queens by his grandparents, an introspective child whose latent creativity kicked into overdrive when his grandfather presented him with twin decks and a mixer. Following investment in Def Jam by Columbia Records, LL Cool J's album *Radio* was released in April 1985 – tracks such as 'You'll Rock' and 'Rock the Bells' combining Cool J's stripped-down b-boy beats and rhymes with a rock aesthetic directly attributable

The Beastie Boys pictured during their 'dumb ass' era.

to Rubin's influence. The album, which cost a mere $7,000 to record, was a massive success and appealed to a wide spectrum of fans. An advocate of accessibility, Cool J stated, 'This music I'm making isn't only for the black kids.' The public agreed. *Radio* went platinum inside four months. Def Jam were about to go glob-al. Both 'I Need a Beat' and *Radio* were hailed as a minimalist progression for hip-hop. While lyrically superficial, the sparse rhythms and the explosive intensity of the cuts were underscored by Rubin's production on *Radio* being credited as 'reduction'.

LL Cool J had been discovered by Beastie Boy Adam Horovitz, who played the young rapper's demo to Rubin. The Beastie Boys were formed as a hardcore punk outfit in 1981. They were comprised initially of teenagers Michael Diamond (Mike D) on vocals and Adam Yauch (MCA) on bass, who had met at a Bad Brains gig in New York, along with guitarist John Berry and drummer Kate Shellenback (later with Luscious Jackson). As a quartet, they released one EP, *Poly Wog Stew*, before splitting. Hardcore bands like Black Flag, Minor Threat and, in particular, Bad Brains heavily influenced the group's original sound. 'Darryl Jenifer [Bad Brains' bassist] is my favourite,' Yauch explained. 'He's the musician who most influenced my playing . . . if you listen to our hardcore tracks, I think you can hear his influ-ence . . . I've seen them [Bad Brains] like 50 times.'

The group reformed two years later with the addition of Adam Horovitz (King Ad Rock), initially as a guitarist. As punk was now dead, this new line-up began experimenting with their sound. The earliest fruit born by these experiments was 'Cookie Puss', a track based around a hoax telephone call that employed rudimentary sampling techniques and foreshadowed the direction the Beasties were to take – despite being intended initially as a joke.

'We got tired of the hardcore scene. It was very negative. The rap scene is a lot better because the rappers all have more camaraderie with each other,' explained Diamond. Adam Yauch identifies the trio's assimilation of both rap and hardcore as 'a New York thing', stressing how 'when we were growing up, clubs wouldn't only play rap or punk or funk – you'd go to hear a hardcore band and they'd play James Brown on the P.A. between the sets.' When Rubin saw potential in the band and quickly signed them to Def Jam, Simmons viewed them with a businessman's eye – seeing the snotty white boys as a means to sell hip-hop to middle America. The Beastie Boys immediately set about refining their raw energy into a cohesive sound.

Thrust before hordes of teeny-boppers on Madonna's Like a Virgin tour, the band came to relish the torrent of abuse directed at them by the adolescent audience. 'It was thousands of screaming girls telling us to get lost,' explains Mike D. The Beasties responded with a hail of insults, flipping the kids the finger and telling them, 'Go fuck yourselves!' When asked about the Beasties' brutally dismissive treatment of her audience, Madonna revealed, 'I just loved them for that.' Russell Simmons also made it his policy to include the group on the bill of any rap shows he promoted, and it was in this often hostile environment that the band described as 'the Three Stooges on acid' honed their stagecraft.

In an interview with *DJ Times*, Mike D outlined his rap influences: 'The first hip-hop I ever heard – really before it was ever on wax – was when I was

A youthful, featherweight LL Cool J from 1985.

going to school hearing kids playing battle tapes. As soon as "Rapper's Delight" or "Flash It to the Beat" by Grandmaster Flash came out, we'd start to request them downtown . . . Another influential DJ was [Afrika] Bambaataa, and that definitely changed the world for us when we heard him spin. First of all he had this presence – not as a performer or someone on stage – but when he came into the place, him and his whole Zulu Nation crew, it was this presence. He just took over the vibe, dominated the vibe, he made the vibe. The thing that really fucked us up was that we expected him to play hip-hop jams. And they did, but the whole shit was mixing in "Apache" or "Son of Scorpio" and then he'd go into the craziest pop record and make it work, like "Oh Micky, you're so fine!" That's what I mean by freakin' it. Bam could mix the most unlikely records and make it work.'

'Black kids are always hipper to what's going on . . . rap music; what's so good

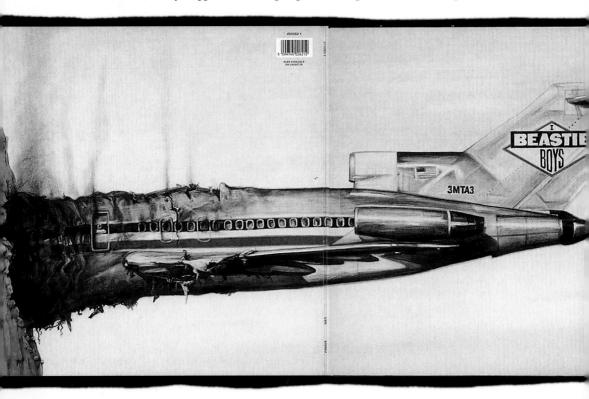

The cover of the Beastie Boys' 1986 debut, Licensed To Ill. *At this stage of their career the Beasties were not unduly concerned with matters of taste.*

about it is that it's always changing. You'll have new rap records on the radio all the time whilst on rock stations they're still playing "Stairway to Heaven". Black stations like Kiss and BLS have these rap hours on Friday and Saturday and it's all new stuff. The rock stations have, like, the New Music Hour and they play Madonna and the Stones album and, y'know it's like "new music" that you're going to hear every day for months . . .' Mike Diamond

The release of their first single, 'Rock Hard', was a musical watershed that defined the band's direction for years to come, sampling AC/DC's classic 'Back in Black' riff overlaid with the Beasties' ersatz white-trash rhymes. Their follow-up release, 'She's on It', was written by Run DMC's Joseph Simmons and Darryl McDaniels and became the group's first significant hit. While adhering to the fusion template created by Run DMC, 'She's on It' took the rock-rap style in a similar direction to 'Rock Hard' and was included on the soundtrack of *Krush Groove*. Distinguishing between the two bands' approaches, Adam Yauch explained, 'Run DMC are coming from growing up in a black neighbourhood and being into black music and they're adding rock . . . We grew up with white music and we're putting rap into it. It's like we're coming from the opposite direction to them.' With their breakthrough chart success behind them, the Beastie Boys were well on their way to establishing themselves as the first significant white rap band.

The Beastie Boys found themselves in suitable company when they joined Run

'I love my culture – I love being black – but it's not something I want to talk about all day.' – LL Cool J

DMC, LL Cool J and Whodini (an old-school rap act) on the Raising Hell tour. 'We have the most mixed group of fans of any tour out there,' enthused Mike D. 'We get an equal share of black kids and white kids, which is what is so great about rock and rap merging.' Initially guaranteed only a twenty-minute opening slot, the Beasties quickly ascended the bill as their popularity increased. The tour also brought the band to Europe for the first time, without any of the controversy that was to engulf their next visit.

'When we first started, a lot of people, not people in the music – a lot of rappers and DJ's have always taken us seriously – but to a lot of people it was just inconceivable for white kids to rap. It was like we'd suddenly decided to become American Indians for a while and live on the reservation. Now we've built up some respect. We definitely broke some ground but we went through

some embarrassing gigs doing it.' Adam Yauch

Originally titled *Don't Be a Faggot, Licensed to Ill* was first made available in May 1986. It was this album that finally cemented the combination of rap and rock elements in an entirely new idiom. Taking the creative influence that Rubin and Simmons had brought to bear on Run DMC and LL Cool J in a new, punkier direction, the album was the highest selling debut LP in Columbia Records' history, proving – as with the Monkees and the Ramones – that dumb sells. The album was swaggering, white middle-class, cock-rock self-aggrandisement. The music was a further extension of Rubin's fusion ethic, this time orientated toward the rock end of the spectrum. The second single taken from the album, 'Fight for Your Right', was almost a straight-up slice of heavy metal save for the rapped vocals, the track that, more than any other from that era, provided the aural template for many contemporary nu-metal acts.

The Beastie Boys soon found themselves at the centre of a media feeding-fren-

'Run DMC are coming from growing up in a black neighbour-hood and being into black music and they're adding rock . . . We grew up with white music and we're putting rap into it.' – Mike D

zy surrounding their 1987 world tour. Employing topless go-go dancers in cages and stage props like a giant hydraulic penis, they came in for shrill criticism from the 'moral majority'. The band were accused of instigating riots and insulting disabled kids at a public appearance, and various other forms of obnoxious behaviour. This furore reached new heights of absurdity when the *Daily Mirror* taboid, looking for a new Sex Pistols to stir their sense of outrage, described the group as 'Every parent's worst nightmare' and repeated the second-hand accusation about them insulting the disabled. But the band were beginning to tire of their image, which had developed an aura of self-parody. No longer wishing to be portrayed as beer-swilling oafs by Def Jam, the trio left with the intention of forming their own label (though they would ultimately sign with Capitol). Simmons was less than impressed with this 'betrayal' and threatened to withhold the Beasties' royalties in revenge for their decampment.

LL Cool J's follow-up to the reductive *Radio* was released in the spring of 1987. The album, *Bigger & Deffer*, often seems like a cynical attempt to incorporate a wide variety of softer mainstream styles in an effort to increase marketablility. 'I'm Bad' and 'Go Cut Creator, Go' represented typical slices of Rubinesque rap-rock,

(with the latter track heavily sampling Chuck Berry). Describ
History of Hip-Hop as 'a concept album, and the concept is LL's ego,' the bulk of
the recording is typical of the swaggering 'brag-hop' that comprised much of his
output. But the self-appointed first sex-god of hip-hop ('LL Cool J' being a trun-
cation of the legend 'Ladies Love Cool James') broke new ground with the track 'I
Need Love' – effectively the first rap ballad, paving the way for a procession of pap-
raps and saccharine boy-bands that would haunt the charts throughout the next
decade. Complete with a nauseating video that featured LL in his limo, pining for
a girl 'as sweet as a dove', 'I Need Love' became a massive hit worldwide. Cool J
took his ascension to Barry White status a little too literally, and was once arrest-
ed for 'public lewdness' after he had mimed fucking a sofa during a stage performance. Ladies do, indeed, love Cool James!

The next major Def Jam release was a significant move away from both the
traditional 'two turntables and a microphone' approach of LL Cool J and the
contrived mayhem of the Beastie Boys. Public Enemy's 1987 debut album,
Yo! Bum Rush the Show, introduced a new, highly politicised form of rap.
Although Rubin was only credited as executive producer (production for the
album handled by Hank Shocklee and the band themselves), the sound owed
more to the minimalist production of *Radio* than the 'stadium rock' style of
the Beastie Boys. The album was a solid seller, acting as a showcase for Public
Enemy's trailblazing potential and political insight.

> '*If Public Enemy wants to do songs about killing whitey, and I'm whitey,
> that's fine, and I'll support them in that attempt, as long as what they do
> is good musically, which is all I really care about. It's only commentary. I
> don't think music can change the world.*' Rick Rubin

In 1988 Def Jam issued the album that was to make Public Enemy the most influential rap act of the decade. *It Takes a Nation of Millions to Hold Us Back* was a
fierce polemical development from the band's debut. Tracks such as 'Bring the
Noise' and 'Night of the Living Baseheads' were multi-layered sonic assaults that
took rap into new, heavier areas almost akin to industrial music. Chuck D's lyrics
espoused a politicised agenda that owed much to the socially-aware funk of the
early 1970's, and continues to resonate through bands such as Rage Against the
Machine and Amen. 'Black Steel in the House of Chaos' was an extraordinary nar-
rative that detailed a spectacular prison breakout and provided an anthem for
incarcerated black youth. The song was also reminiscent of Malcolm X's assertion
that to be a black American was, in itself, a form of imprisonment. Key to Public

Public Enemy: Yo! Bum Rush
The Show *(1987) created both
musical and political shockwaves.*

Enemy's distinctive sound
was their DJ, Terminator X,
whose radical subversion of
scratching and cutting techniques produced a relentless
aural soundscape of sirens,
beats and samples that has
directly influenced contemporary mix-masters like Sid
Wilson of Slipknot. The
album also featured the metal
samples now synonymous
with Def Jam, 'She Watch
Channel Zero?!' being an immense slice of heavy rock that overlaid Public Enemy's
aural assault.

The band, described by vocalist Chuck D as 'the Led Zeppelin of rap', appropriated a paramilitary chic. This Black Panther-esque image was juxtaposed with the
appearance of D's vocal partner Flavor Flav, who adopted the persona of a jester –
strutting about the stage with a kitchen-wall clock hanging from his neck, mugging,
and injecting hip one-liners into D's more astute polemic. Public Enemy's first
major tour was an opening slot for the Beastie Boys. The band were musically
unprepared for the exposure, and were compelled to lip-sync over studio recordings,
meeting with a puzzled reaction from audience and critics alike. Writing for
Penthouse in 1987, Timothy White spectacularly missed the point of Public Enemy
altogether, by concentrating upon the verbal belligerence of their lyrics while ignor-
ing their political and moral context: 'Flavor Flav and Chuck D spew boastful bile
about gang violence . . . and the pleasures of misogyny . . . This is black rap at its
grimmest, an invitation to stomp on tombstones and tenement corpses.'

The radical stance of the group was amplified by links with the Nation of
Islam fundamentalist church, of which both Terminator X and the Security of the
First World (the band's paramilitary-style dance troupe) organiser Professor Griff
were members. This extremist stance led the media to criticise the band for their
endorsement of Nation of Islam minister Louis Farrakhan, who was vilified by the
American press for anti-Semitism. Chuck D consistently denied such sentiments,
stating that Public Enemy simply wanted to present Black nationalist politics to

their disenfranchised audience. However, Chuck D was ultimately urged by Def Jam to sack Griff for remarks that hinted at a global Jewish conspiracy.

While Public Enemy were criticised by some activists for presenting 'politics as theatre', their revolutionary look and sound attracted plaudits from prominent media figures such as Will Smith ('What [Public Enemy] are doing is trying to uplift the black youth') and Spike Lee, director of *She's Gotta Have It* and *School Daze*. Lee used Public Enemy's music as both an incidental and central aspect of his brilliant 1989 film *Do the Right Thing*. The exposure boosted the band's profile, with the film's theme song, 'Fight the Power', becoming a massive hit, despite its attacks on such white cultural icons as Elvis Presley and John Wayne. The success of the band was a relief to Def Jam co-founder Russell Simmons, who had originally been sceptical of Public Enemy's merits. Rick Rubin recalls Simmons' initial reaction: 'Russell said, "You're wasting your time. This is black punk rock. This is garbage. You could make pop records, why are you wasting your time on Public Enemy?" I said, "Because they're the greatest group in the world. Because the pop records are the ones that aren't important. *This* is what's important."'

As the 1980's ended Simmons and Rubin were pulling in different creative

'What [Public Enemy] are doing is trying to uplift the black youth.'
– Will Smith

directions. While Rubin held fast to his rock-rap ideal, Simmons felt the need to diversify into more traditional black music forms such as soul and R'n'B. Rubin signed the death-metal band Slayer to the label, grafting elements of the rap aesthetic to their music in the unlikeliest expansion of the fusion ethos yet. This direction did not meet with Simmons' approval. Rubin also became embroiled in a legal wrangle with the Beastie Boys, which ultimately led to his leaving the label to form Def American Records. However, he was able to dissolve Def Jam's innovative partnership without acrimony, as he describes: 'Russell and I were going in different directions both musically and business-wise. And I thought that being as we were good friends, it would be better for us to break off and still be able to be friends, instead of some day hating each other . . . So I said, "Do you want to leave?" And he said, "No" and I said, "OK, fine, I'll leave." And we're still friends.' Subsequently, the Beastie Boys moved to Capitol Records to produce the acclaimed but slow-selling second album *Paul's Boutique*. Simmons continues to manage the label, having revived its fortunes in the mid-1990's with such acts as Onyx, DMX and Jay-Z.

The chart success of *Apocalypse '91* has since proven to be Public Enemy's last hur-

rah. An album of B-sides and studio out-takes – *Greatest Misses* (1993) – was issued to a lukewarm reception, while the following year's new offering, *Muse Sick-n-Hour Message*, was almost universally panned and failed to sell in any great quantities. Flavor Flav made headlines in the daily papers more often than in the music press, his frequent arrests for drugs and violence becoming a problem for the band and their label. Public Enemy broke up in 1994, with Chuck D departing to pursue solo projects (including a memoir entitled *Fight the Power*), while Terminator X headed for South Carolina to farm ostriches. However, in 1998 the band reformed with their original line-up to record the soundtrack for the 1998 Spike Lee 'joint' *He Got Game.* Chuck D had found less overtly political targets for his rage in the form of the record industry, and enraged Def Jam by offering unreleased Public Enemy material on the band's website. It led to the band parting company with their label, the delighted D declaring he felt 'like a black man in 1866, trying to figure out what the fuck I do with my freedom.'
LL Cool J remained loyal to Def Jam, recording a series of albums that were mod-

Public Enemy – the shock troops of hip-hop.

erately successful if bland. 1989's *Walking with a Panther* was very much a case of the wrong subject matter at the wrong time, with the apolitical Cool J crooning about jewellery and posing with the eponymous big cat for publicity pictures, while Public Enemy were invoking the spirit of an entirely different type of panther. Explaining his *laissez-faire* attitude to socio-political issues, Cool J disclosed, 'I love my culture – I love being black – but it's not something I want to talk about all day.' This non-confrontational attitude has enabled Cool J to penetrate the white suburbs of middle America in a way that Public Enemy or NWA could never do. His subsequent albums, *Mama Said Knock You Out, Fourteen Shots to the Dome, Mr Smith* and *Phenomenon*, were radio-friendly rap, and it was perhaps unsurprising that he was invited to attend Bill Clinton's 1993 inauguration as the event's token rapper. Recently, LL has diversified from music, writing an autobiography entitled *I Make My Own Rules*, appearing in the NBC sitcom *In the House*, and establishing himself as a movie actor in such films as *Halloween: H20* and *Deep Blue Sea*.

'I don't know why but I just like that Funkadelic guitar; I like to rock out on it.' – Adam Horovitz

Throughout the 1990's the Beastie Boys continued to draw upon a diverse spectrum of musical influences, from hardcore and rap to swing, jazz and funk. The band returned to traditional instruments for their third album, *Check Your Head*, producing a hard-edged fusion between rap, punk and funk that was heavily influenced by the P-Funk sound of twenty years earlier. 'I listen to a lot of Eddie Hazel [Parliament/Funkadelic guitarist] and Jimi Hendrix,' explained Adam Horovitz. 'I don't know why but I just like that Funkadelic guitar; I like to rock out on it.' The band's image has moved further away from the drunken excesses of the *Licensed to Ill* era, and, by the time their hugely successful fourth album *Ill Communication* was released, had completed a transition from boozed-up frat boys to urbane hipsters.

The Red Hot Chili Peppers: Anthony Kiedis, Flea, Chad Smith, John Frusciante.

GUILTY PARTIES
Rock and Rap

'We don't necessarily sound black or white.
We sound like people connected to a universal energy,
inspired to play music that knows no colour.'
– Anthony Kiedis, the Red Hot Chili Peppers

As increasing numbers of rap acts mined rock music's back catalogue of guitar riffs, it was hardly a surprise when the process reversed and rock groups assimilated aspects of rap. In the same year that Run DMC hit big with *King of Rock* (1985), San Francisco quintet Faith No More produced their debut album *We Care a Lot* – described by *Rolling Stone* as an 'innovative sound, a mixture of rock, rap and heavy metal.'

We Care a Lot was the first album of its kind to attract attention from the international music media. However, the band were by no means the originators of this strain of fusion, but one of a number of experimental West Coast bands, formed in the early 1980's, who sought to expand the boundaries of heavy metal. Chief among these were the Red Hot Chili Peppers, who had been performing a hybrid of rock, rap, punk and funk around the Los Angeles circuit since 1983. Originally comprised of Anthony Kiedis on vocals, Michael 'Flea' Balzary on bass, Hillel Slovak on guitar and Jack Irons on drums, the Chili Peppers built a formidable live reputation based on their upbeat hardcore sensibility. As a homage to their punk roots, the band regularly took the stage to the Clash's 'London Calling', but the RHCP sound was essentially defined by Flea's virtuoso funk-bass rhythms. As a huge admirer of P-Funk legend Bootsy Collins, Flea emulated the slap-bass technique of both Collins and Sly and the Family Stone bassist Larry Graham. A consummate musician, it was Flea's diversity of influences (ranging from Miles Davis and Muddy Waters through to the Velvet Underground and Black Flag) that contributed most to the quartet's experimentalism. Flea was musically attracted to all kinds of cross cultural fusions, particularly those that presented funk within a rock framework.

The innovative bassist cites post-punk agit-funkers the Gang of Four as a specific influence, recalling that, 'The first time I heard the *Entertainment* record, listening to the razor sharp rhythms . . . The little Flea's mind was blown. It completely changed the way I looked at rock music and sent me on my trip as a bass player.'

Despite the critical acclaim received by their first two albums (a self-titled debut and the George Clinton-produced *Freaky Styley*), the group had to wait until 1989, after the smack-induced death of guitarist Slovak, before enjoying commercial success with their fourth LP, *Mother's Milk*. MTV, who previously held firm prejudices against rap music, showed no such reluctance in presenting rappin' white boys to a global audience. This propelled the Chili Peppers toward massive worldwide sales, which peaked with the 1991 album *BloodSugarSexMagik,* produced by Rick Rubin (its featured single, 'Give It Away', remains a staple of MTV scheduling to this day).

The lesson was not lost on Faith No More, who, in 1989, dismissed vocalist Chuck Mosley in favour of Mr. Bungle frontman Mike Patton, who had shown adeptness at switching between traditional rock and rap vocals. The band's 1989 single 'Epic' was tailormade for the newly-receptive MTV. It was a huge hit, with the subsequent album, *Blind Faith*, going platinum. However, the group found it impossible to follow up on this success, recording two more albums before finally splitting in 1998.

'The first time I saw them, I'd never heard of them. This was at a time they were playing so fast you couldn't even tell what they were playing, it was just a blur.' – Rick Rubin

Like the Chili Peppers, Slayer (along with funk-metallers Fishbone) were part of the eclectic LA metal scene of the time. The band were – alongside Metallica and the turgid Megadeth – amongst the pioneers of speed metal, the sub-genre that spliced the velocity and aggression of punk to the bombast of heavy metal. Rick Rubin recounts his first encounter with the band: 'The first time I saw them, I'd never heard of them. This was at a time they were playing so fast you couldn't even tell what they were playing, it was just a blur. But the command they had of the audience, I'd never seen anything like it.'

Since their formation in 1982, the quartet had built a reputation for the intensity of their live performances, and, by 1986, had recorded a magnum opus album, *Reign in Blood*, blisteringly brief at only 28 minutes long and produced by Rick Rubin. However, Rubin's influence did not lead the band into rock/rap crossover

Slayer: masters of metal, mayhem and murder, at the altar.

territory, despite their being signed to Def Jam. The album contained none of his usual evangelical cross-pollination, being simply a refined explosion of breakneck thrash. It also generated some controversy due to 'Angel of Death', a lyric about Nazi doctor Joseph Mengele, compounded when a magazine article quoted the band themselves espousing right-wing attitudes toward 'matters of society and justice' – in particular, an enthusiasm for the death penalty.

The band's first contact with the hip-hop scene happened by chance, when Rubin required a guitar lead for the Beastie Boys' *License to Ill* album. Slayer guitarist Kerry King was on hand: 'We were in the studio at the same time and I didn't even know any of them,' admits King. 'They were on Def Jam and they needed a lead and I went, "OK!" and went down there and did it and that was it. I did get to be in their video which was cool because we didn't have any videos at the time.' Slayer finally ventured into the rap arena proper with their 1994 cover of Edinburgh punk band the Expoited's 'Disorder', which they recorded with Ice T for the *Judgement Night* soundtrack.

Also expanding out of the speed/thrash-metal ghetto were Anthrax, a New York foursome who adopted a more extreme posture after starting out with the standard eighties heavy metal formula. Their debut album, *Fistful of Metal,* (1984) featured a wilfully Spinal Tap-esque sleeve, indicating a tendency toward self-par-

The sleeve from Anthrax's crossover hit, 'I'm the Man'.

ody – this quasi-satirical approach emphasised by a side project called SOD (Stormtroopers of Death) that featured three quarters of the group, issuing the startlingly-entitled *Speak English or Die* in 1985.

Anthrax began experimenting with rap by introducing the tongue-in-cheek encore 'I'm the Man' as a regular feature of their live shows. The overwhelmingly positive response encouraged the band to diversify. Vocalist Joey Belladonna says of the song, ' Scott [Ian – Anthrax rhythm guitar/vocals] and them all, they're all into rap and stuff, and they wanted to do a rap song of some sort. The chorus came from the movie *Easy Money*. When the guy says, "I am the man." We got the chorus from that. I just figured on doing something a little different. It was kinda risky at first, and we thought about doing it. I, myself, was a little sceptical about it 'cause . . . ya don't know how the kids are gonna react, we kinda did it humorous enough so that it was funny. We weren't making fun of anything. Some people got the impression we were making fun of black people, or rap.' However, the hiring of black jazz-funk metallers Living Colour as support on their UK tour clearly demonstrated their expanding musical horizons.

Anthrax were an entirely apolitical band who fuse(purely musical reasons. But they made a *faux pas* with (song 'Antisocial', originally recorded by neo-Nazi skinhe their defence, Anthrax were oblivious to the song's explained, 'Charlie [Benante – drums] and them all like 1 ......ng only heard the 1979 cover version by the French rockers of that name. 'I did that one in French, too', he observed, having believed the French translation to be the original lyrics.

> 'A good song should make you tap your foot and get with your girl. A *great* song should destroy cops and set fire to the suburbs. I'm only interested in writing great songs.'
> – Tom Morello

In 1991, Anthrax took the fusion of rock and rap a stage further by touring with Public Enemy. It was the first time that major acts from both camps had shared tour billing, its success leading the two outfits to collaborate on a hit version of Public Enemy's 'Bring the Noise'. As Ian explains of Anthrax's typically relaxed motivation, 'We're fans of them. We decided it would be a fun thing to do. That's it.' '"Bring the Noise" is one of the most incredible live songs ever', new vocalist John Bush, the eventual replacement for Belladonna, later opined. 'Sometimes I sit back and just freak on how crazy the crowd goes on that song. When we were touring with [intense metal behemoths] Pantera, it was like the highlight of the whole fuckin' show for any band.'

While Faith No More are no more, and the Red Hot Chili Peppers have been reincarnated as a laid-back Southern California supergroup, there is no denying either band's influence at the grassroots of rap-rock. As Rage Against the Machine guitarist Tom Morello attests, 'I have nothing but the utmost respect for both of these bands . . . One of the things that was so radical about those bands was that they were combining elements of black music – overtly funky George Clinton/Parliament-style rhythms – with elements of hard rock and punk. That was absolute commercial suicide! At the time the colour barrier was insurmountable. That is something that both of those bands should be commended for.'

Like Public Enemy, Rage Against the Machine, by their very name, positioned themselves in opposition to the forces of tyranny and oppression. The quartet – Tom Morello (guitar), Zack de la Rocha (vocals), Tim Commerford (bass) and Brad Wilk (drums) – established a reputation for combining radical left-wing tivism with blisteringly polemical performances and recordings. It's a testimony to their integrity that they largely sidestepped accusations of sucking hard on corporate dick when signing for the Sony subsidiary Epic Records.

Since their formation in 1991, Rage Against the Machine attacked government oppression, cultural imperialism, racism and censorship. More tangibly, the group provided vocal and financial support to causes such as the sweatshop exploitation of garment workers, the campaigns to free imprisoned political activists Mumia Abu-Jamal and Leonard Peltier, and the Mexican Zapatista freedom fighters. Guitarist and band spokesman Tom Morello was acutely aware of the opportunities presented by the band's status, particularly in terms of publicising injustice and corruption: 'I feel that RATM has operated like a guerrilla radio station,' he claimed, 'broadcasting communiqués from behind enemy lines since 1991.' The group experienced their first brush with controversy on a European tour supporting Suicidal Tendencies, when a cache of t-shirts – demonstrating (to CIA standard) the correct method for constructing Molotov cocktails – was seized and destroyed by anxious French customs officers.

> '"Bring the Noise" is one of the most incredible live songs ever . . . Sometimes I sit back and just freak on how crazy the crowd goes on that song.' – John Bush

Morello, a Harvard graduate and the nephew of former Kenyan president Jomo Kenyatta, formed the group with frontman de La Rocha and drummer Wilk. Both musicians had been active on the LA scene – de la Rocha had formerly fronted punk ensemble Inside Out, while Wilk had previously worked with Eddie Vedder of Pearl Jam. The quartet was finalised with the addition of bassist Commerford, a long-standing friend of de la Rocha.

After playing their first gig in an Orange County living room, the band self-produced a twelve-track cassette including 'Bullet in the Head', which later became their first hit. The tape was constructed around the now familiar RATM formula of rapped and bellowed vocals, hip-hop rhythms and innovative guitar effects. Distributed at live shows, and through the already blossoming fan club, it rapidly sold 5,000 copies.

The cultural clash between rap and rock was defined by Morello in terms of his influences: 'I always loved the huge riffs of Led Zeppelin and Black Sabbath, but, with few exceptions, I thought the lyrical content was lacking. I mean, some of that mystical Celtic "goblin lore" is a bit much . . . it didn't have much to do with my suburban existence. Then there's Public Enemy, who are lyrically brilliant and

The cover of arch polemicists Rage Against the Machine's 1992 debut album featured the self-immolation of a Buddhist monk in protest at the Vietnam conflict.

totally radical. To me that was the missing ingredient, and we cross-bred those two ingredients in a way that felt very natural.'

The key element of Rage Against the Machine's sound was the inventive manner in which Morello used his guitar to produce effects similar to the scratching and cutting of contemporary hip-hop DJ's. As he explained, 'I was really excited by the prospect of playing hip-hop music within the context of a punk rock band, and I wasn't going to make any excuses for there not being a DJ! At the time my chief influences were Terminator X (Public Enemy) and Jam Master J (Run DMC), and I was determined to recreate the record scratching DJ stuff on my guitar.'

Epic Records, not knowing how to interpret RATM's diverse sound, initially marketed them as a rap act, leading the group to tour extensively with Cypress Hill and House of Pain. During this period, the group established their anti-establishment credentials by voicing support for the pro-abortion Rock for Choice and Fairness and Accuracy in Reporting campaigns, and were described by radical hardcore performer Henry Rollins as 'the most happening band in the US'. Rage Against the Machine's eagerly awaited, self-titled debut album was released, to much critical acclaim, in June 1992. The album immediately entered the Top 50 and was lauded by *Billboard* editor-in-chief Timothy White as 'original and virtuosic'. To complement the musical pyrotechnics, the album incorporated plenty of polemical lyrics, particularly 'Killing in the Name of' – its anthemic refrain, 'fuck you, I won't do what you told me,' becoming a rallying call for the band's growing audience of disenfranchised youth.

Released in 1999, The Battle of Los Angeles *was to be Rage Against the Machine's final assault on the evils of capitalism.*

As Morello asserted, the band were happy to be seen as radicals: 'Rage is a band that stands proudly in the domain of bands like the MC5, the Clash and Public Enemy. The MC5 were one of the first overtly revolutionary bands, and I found that to be extraordinary and inspirational. Rage Against the Machine's music is an exclusive product of the band's chemistry . . . Our audiences have hip-hop, hardcore punk and heavy metal contingents, all of whom find elements of our music attractive. For a band like ours, one with a revolutionary outlook, it's great that we can address different groups of people with our music and crash down the barriers that separate different genres.'

'I feel that RATM has operated like a guerrilla radio station broadcasting communiqués from behind enemy lines.' – Tom Morello

The success of *Rage Against the Machine* was accelerated by constant airings of the 'Freedom' video by MTV. However, this level of mass-media exposure was accompanied by pressure for the band to conform to marketing strictures. A radio edit of 'Killing' was produced, effectively castrating the lyric by removing its expletives, de la Rocha commenting that it 'completely shut down the whole purpose of that song'. In July 1993, the group mounted a protest against this censorship by standing naked (save for duct tape, symbolically applied to their mouths) and silent for fifteen long minutes at the opening of their set on the Lollapalooza III tour.

The cliché of the 'difficult' second album proved more than apt to RATM. It was not until Easter 1996 that *Evil Empire* was finally released to an expectant public. The band had hardly disappeared from sight during this recording hiatus, with regular live performances, benefit gigs and television exposure (during early 1994, 'Freedom' was the top-rated video in the US Broadcast and Cable chart) all reinforcing their profile. Days prior to the release of the new album, the band whipped up a healthy storm of controversy during a *Saturday Night Live* filming by hanging US flags the wrong way up over their amplifiers. NBC pulled the plug on Rage's performance at the end of the first song, but the desired affect was achieved: *Evil Empire* entered the *Billboard* chart at number one.

Timothy White reviewed the new album in glowing terms, encapsulating RATM's sound as 'beautifully articulated torrents of hardcore bedlam and humming murals of din'. Named after Ronald Reagan's hysterical description of the Soviet Union, *Evil Empire* represented only a slight development upon the style and content of its predecessor, hitting the same targets in the same manner. But this proved to be exactly what the band's fan-base were waiting for. Allied with impressive promo videos ('Bulls on Parade' was a 1996 MTV Awards nominee in the

Despite splitting up in 2001, Rage Against the Machine have remained enduringly popular and influential.

Rage Against the Machine: Tom Morello, Zack de la Rocha, Brad Wilk, Tim Commerford.

Best Hard Rock Performance category), the group remained the rebels of choice for discerning American dissidents. Speaking to *Alternative Press,* Morello encapsulated his creative ethos: 'A good song should make you tap your foot and get with your girl. A *great* song should destroy cops and set fire to the suburbs. I'm only interested in writing great songs.'

During late 1996-early 1997, Rage continued what Wilk described as 'further raising consciousness' by embarking on an extensive touring schedule and supporting the new counter-culture station Radio Free LA with live appearances, broadcast by over 50 US commercial radio stations. Supporting the band on the US tour were hardcore rappers the Wu-Tang Clan, described by Morello as 'the least commercial, least radio friendly, most raw hip-hop group on the planet.' Regrettably, despite having the number one album of the day, the Wu-Tang received a less than enthusiastic reception and withdrew from the tour at the end of the first week.

The Battle of Los Angeles was to prove the band's final album of original material, emerging in November 1999. Despite criticism that the quartet were rehashing old ideas, in terms of both content and attitude, the album was well received and once again entered the *Billboard* chart at number one. Certainly, the album continued to wear the band's radical politics on its sleeve: 'Guerrilla Radio' referred to the questionable imprisonment of Mumia Abu-Jamal, while the video for 'Sleep Now in the Fire' intelligently satirised consumer culture by presenting sweatshop labourers (instead of dancers) in a direct parody of Gap's vapid clothing ads. Similarly, the band continued to fund causes allied to their beliefs. Morello explained the group's policy of questioning the justice of the US legal system, particularly relating to capital punishment: 'In the United States justice costs money – that's why there are zero rich people on death row.' However, in songs such as 'Mic Check' the band incorporated elements of hip-hop with greater fluidity than on *Rage* or *Evil Empire,* demonstrating their progression toward a more flexible sound.

'For a band like ours, one with a revolutionary outlook, it's great that we can address different groups of people with our music and crash down the barriers that separate different genres.' – Tom Morello

Despite Morello's assertion to the RATM fan club that 'there's no reason why the next record can't top even *The Battle of Los Angeles*', the group effectively dissolved following de la Rocha's abrupt departure to pursue a solo career. Although the remaining trio were believed to have considered replacing him with former Soundgarden vocalist Chris Cornell (with whom they ultimately went on to form Audioslave), the final release from the 'alternative medium for young people' proved to be *Renegades* – a collection of covers recorded before the split featuring songs originally performed by acts such as Afrika Bambaataa, Minor Threat, Cypress Hill and the Stooges. While the album included some enjoyable material, it was a less than fitting epitaph to a band largely defined by their political radicalism. Even post-break-up, Rage Against the Machine have retained their status as the archetypal anti-establishment band. This was demonstrated by the CIA's shutting down of the RATM website message board, citing the 'un-American content' of some of the postings.

A Xavante tribesman adorns the cover of Sepultura's ethnically orientated album Roots *(1996).*

URBAN SHAKEDOWN
Diversification and Fusion

'In Brazil, life is cheap.' – Max Cavalera, Sepultura

In the wake of Rage Against the Machine's success, and in keeping with the prevailing ethos of experimentation that characterised early 1990s underground metal, a new cadre of rap-metal fusion pioneers emerged, bringing fresh, diverse elements to the mix.

Often unfairly characterised as one-dimensional and lowbrow, Biohazard spoke for the disenfranchised. Lyrically, the Brooklyn foursome concentrated upon the harsh realities of the inner city (an established staple of both punk and rap), while their music was an immense sonic clash between hardcore metal guitar and beatbox rhythms replicated with a drum-kit. Founder Billy Graziadei describes his influences as 'anything with a heavy beat . . . from the Bad Brains to Beethoven to Black Sabbath and hip-hop.' As befits a band who characterise themselves as the underdog, their initial history was a morass of contractual wrangling, culminating in departure from their first label, Maze. Through constant live work, the quartet of Graziadei (guitar/vocals), Evan Seinfeld (bass/vocals), Bobby Hambel (guitar) and Danny Schuler (drums) had established a loyal fan base that encouraged the influential Roadrunner label (later home to Slipknot, Fear Factory and Sepultura) to sign them for 1992's *Urban Discipline*.

'Radio won't play us much because we curse all the time . . . but that's the way we fucking talk.' – Billy Graziadei

Recorded in less than a fortnight, with minimal financial backing, the album cemented the group's live reputation for taking rap-metal into more hardcore areas. While Vanilla Ice presented a white middle-class pastiche of urban rap, Biohazard presented life 'How It Is Y'all'. This uncompromising approach provoked the inevitable parental backlash. 'Radio won't play us much because we curse all the time,' Billy Graziadei complained in a fanzine interview, 'but that's

Biohazard's 1995 album, Urban Discipline.

the way we fucking talk.'

Following collaboration with hardcore rappers Onyx (a version of their hit 'Slam' for the *Judgement Night* sound-track, the video of which became a staple of MTV's *Headbanger's Ball*), the band signed with Warner to record *State of the World Address* in 1994. Featuring a characteris-tically heavy production by Ed Stasium (known for his work with the Ramones, Ratt, Living Colour and Motorhead), the album reasserted the band's hardcore musical principles and was universally well received. After the band parted company with guitarist Bobby Hambel in the mid-1990s, the 1996 release of *Mata Leao* failed to entice a larger audience despite positive fan reaction to the tighter, more controlled sound of the stripped-down band. Hambel was sub-sequently replaced by former Helmet axeman Rob Echeverria.

Unsuccessful dalliance with a less aggressive sound and a lack of massive com-mercial success has left the group's commitment and passion undiminished. As Evan Seinfield puts it, 'Would you rather have a million fans for a year, or a hun-dred-thousand for ten?' Biohazard are sustained by their loyal fan base to the extent where they have to make few compromises. 'We are survivors,' insists Seinfield, lending sincerity to the cliché. 'We do what we gotta do to live.'

Like Biohazard, Dog Eat Dog also originated from New York City (Manhattan, in their case). However, despite generic similarities, their approach to rap-metal fusion was set in a distinctly upbeat groove – drawing upon elements of metal, punk, hip-hop and reggae. As vocalist John Connor stressed, 'Just because we have roots in hardcore, doesn't mean we're limiting ourselves.' Having released an EP entitled *Warrant* in 1994, DED's full-length debut, *All Boro Kings* (featuring con-tributions from Bad Brains' Darryl Jenifer), became a surprise global hit, pro-pelling the group towards the 1995 MTV Breakthrough Artist of the Year Award.

Despite criticism that the quartet (John Connor on vocals, Dave Nearbore on bass, Sean Kilkenny on guitar, and Brandon Finlay on drums) were derivative of

Rage Against the Machine, among others, the band were more in keeping with the blunt-smokin' attitude of rap acts such as Cypress Hill and Onyx. Produced by RZA, previously responsible for structuring the Wu-Tang Clan's distinctive aural assault, DED's follow up album *Play Games* proved less successful (possibly due to the lack of anthemic stompers like its predecessor's 'No Fronts' and 'Who's the King?'). Undaunted by this, and despite personnel changes that led to the band reforming under the 'All Boro Kings' name, the band remain resolutely positive in their approach. As John Connor explained to the Iconofan Network site, 'Dog Eat Dog is a party band, our music is celebration . . .'

'Would you rather have a million fans for a year, or a hundred-thousand for ten?' – Evan Seinfeld

Described by MTV journalist John Bartelson as 'riding the line between hip-hop and funk-punk', Philadelphia-based ensemble the Goats' second album, *No Goats No Glory*, landed them squarely in rap-metal territory. Pitched stylistically between the Beastie Boys (whom they supported on tour), Cypress Hill and New York Jewish rappers 3rd Bass, the Goats moved away from the more politically-orientated content of their first recording, *Tricks of the Shade*, toward a more upbeat, hedonistic outlook. Employing a loose mix of rap, funk, jazz and howling metal riffs, *No Goats* was a ramshackle landscape of cultural diversity, featuring an eight-minute aural montage comprised of dialogue, music and sound effects samples, and a collaboration with Bad Brains (on the final track, 'Idiot Business') that reworked George Clinton's 'Cosmic Slop' as ragga-metal.

Also drawing inspiration from the fast-talk delivery of ragga were Dub War, a quartet from Newport. Aside from being the first Welsh dub-metal act to achieve any kind of popularity, the band continued a lineage of fusing Jamaican and western protest music that had its origins in the punk-reggae stylings of the Clash, the Slits and photographer Dennis Morris's seminal dub-rockers Basement 5. Fronted by the energetic Benji, who had served a dancehall apprenticeship under eighties dub legend the Mad Professor, the group made a significant impact at the Glastonbury festival in Britain and Holland's Dynamo festival and with their 1995 debut album on the Dub War label: a raw fusion of punk, metal and ragga entitled *Pain*.

However, the band's subsequent releases revealed a softer edge that indicated their future direction. 'I've never seen why we should stick to one style when there's so much music to enjoy,' insisted Benji, looking on it as a natural maturing process. But the band failed to imprint itself on the global consciousness, and ultimately split

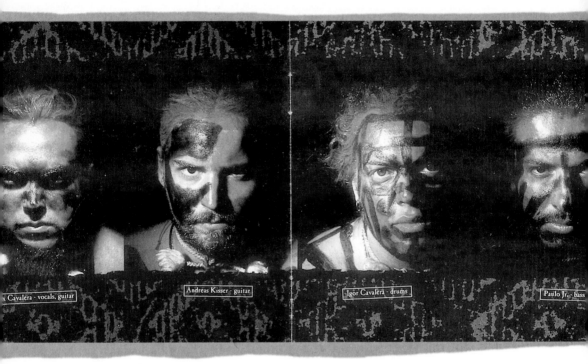

Sepultura: Max Cavalera, Andreas Kisser, Igor Cavalera, Paulo Junior.

during 1999. Subsequent to a guest slot on Soulfly's debut album, Benji has resurfaced (along with former members of Dub War) with a new band, Skindred.

For their part, Brazilian thrash monolith Sepultura brought their own ethnicity to the boiling metal fusion stew. Formed by brothers Max and Igor Cavalera in Belo Horizonte during the mid-eighties, the band had built a solid reputation in their homeland and, following the replacement of their original guitarist Jairo T by Andreas Kisser, released their second full-length recording, *Schizophrenia*. The album drew the attention of a wider audience and persuaded Roadrunner to sign them up.

The first three albums recorded by Sepultura for their new label – *Beneath the Remains* (1989), *Arise* (1991) and *Chaos AD* (1993) – progressively assimilated elements from outside their immediate musical sphere. 'A lot of metal bands are really afraid of experimenting, bringing in new elements to their music,' described Igor Cavalera, 'and I think with that, you're losing a lot of the spirit of always challenging yourself.' (Despite their growing instrumental proficiency, however, the band sacrificed none of their trademark ear-splitting sonic attack or politically-charged lyrics.) Drawing upon such disparate influences as African tribal music and traditional South American Indian rhythms, *Chaos AD* was greeted with critical acclaim and propelled into the *Billboard* Top 40. Major tours with Ozzy Osbourne, Pantera and Al Jourgensen's industrial-hardcore behemoth Ministry cemented Sepultura's reputation as potent live performers.

With the release of *Roots* in 1996, the group were seen to extensively mine their own rich cultural heritage. Venturing into central Brazil, the group lived among the Xavante tribe, a people who had only been in contact with 'civilisation' for less than 50 years. 'Most of the white people that went there were studying them [the Xavante],' explained Igor, 'and doing research on what they were about, so they had no relation with them . . . so with us, they were really happy to have us there, because we were not there to treat them as freaks . . . it was just music. The [cultural and musical] exchange.'

'A lot of metal bands are really afraid of experimenting, bringing in new elements to their music, and I think with that, you're losing a lot of the spirit of always challenging yourself.' – Igor Cavalera

Produced by Ross Robinson (who had previously overseen Korn's groundbreaking debut), *Roots* featured tracks such as 'Ratamahatta' and the thirteen-minute 'Itsari' – a percussive tour de force featuring Xavante musician/priest Carlinhos Brown, recorded in a canyon near the Indigo Ranch studio in Malibu. The album represented a creative high-water mark for the band. While its title track enticed the less adventurous fan toward the band's cross-cultural experimentation, *Roots* achieved massive worldwide sales and succeeded in introducing traditional Third World music to the pre-millennial rock audience. Following disagreements over the way the band was managed (by Max Cavalera's wife, Gloria), Max left Sepultura to form Soulfly. The remaining trio enlisted former Overfiend vocalist Derrick Green and have struggled to repeat their former successes, without the fearsome vocal and writing talent of their departed frontman.

To the NRA and the religious right, Ice-T represented the unacceptable face of urban music.

THE LAST MOTHERFUCKER
Ice-T and Body Count

'I really don't think our record is any more controversial than any other rock group. We're just black.' – Ice-T

When Ice-T (formerly the less macho-sounding Tracy Morrow) released the track 'Body Count' at the end of his 1991 *OG: Original Gangster* album, it seemed like just another example of the ongoing process of rap/rock fusion. However, the rapper subsequently took the bold step of forming a full-blown rock band named after the landmark track. Comprised of fellow former students from Ice's South Central LA alma mater, Crenshaw High School, the side-project band joined their originator on the 1991 Lollapalooza tour.

Comprised of guitarists Ernie-C and D-Roe and rhythm section Mooseman (bass) and Beatmaster V (drums), the quintet performed a well-received fifteen-minute encore at the end of Ice-T's main set. Inspired by this positive response from the rock-orientated audience and opening slots with incongruous old-school metal roadmates Guns 'N Roses and Metallica, as well as an extended tour with hardcore ensembles DRI and ProPain, the Ice decided to release a full-blown album with the rap-metal ensemble. Having already carved out an acting career (appearing in and contributing to the soundtrack of *New Jack City*) and published the anti-censorship tract *The Iceberg/Freedom of Speech . . . Just Watch What You Say*, the idea of branching out in a new musical direction held no fears for the renaissance MC. The new band was also seen as a means to escape the media-generated hysteria surrounding rap concerts: 'hardcore rap has run into a stonewall where it's hard to get the venues, 'cause the media's hyped it up into every time we have a concert someone gets killed, which is bullshit.'

In a comprehensive interview with *Convulsion* magazine, Ice-T explained the genesis of the Body Count dynamic: 'The guys that play on Body Count are the guys that play the live instruments on my albums, like in "Girl Tried to Kill Me" there was a live guitar, that was Ernie C, [there are] a few basslines, once in a while you hear a live

Ice-T's brand of uncompromising rap-metal courted controversy, and usually found it.

drum. So these are my boys, so they're always fightin' with me about putting more rock on the album and I'm like, "Well come on, this is rap." I wanna do it . . . so I was like, "Fuck it, let's make a metal group, and we're gonna call it Body Count, and I'm gonna be the lead singer and we're just going to be the alter-ego of Ice-T.'"

The self-titled LP was released in 1992, showcasing a sound accessible to both the metal and hip-hop camps that the rapper described as 'a cross between Slayer and Motorhead – Motorhead is a groove group, and Slayer is aggressive. What I try to call it is consumable metal.' *Body Count* ran head long into a maelstrom of controversy, largely fuelled by the censorious rage of right-wing gun lobbyist and veteran actor Charlton Heston – who found this particular flava of metal less than consumable. Heston took umbrage at the album's 'KKK Bitch' and 'Cop Killer', the lyrics of which postulated a violent response to the prolonged assault visited upon Rodney King by the LAPD: 'I know your family's grieving/but tonight we get even,' declaimed Ice to the dead cop he depicted as the focus of black rage. 'FUCK 'EM!' barked the backing vocals to the mention of an LAPD officer's relatives. Heston harangued the board of Time-Warner (the band's label, Sire's, parent company) with a fire-and-brimstone sermon. Combined with the threat of a George Bush/Oliver North-sanctioned boycott, it caused the label to panic. Sire refused to support any of Ice-T's future projects (rap, metal or otherwise) unless the track was withdrawn from the album. Locked into his recording contract, the rapper had little option but to acquiesce and the offending track was replaced by a spoken-word piece featuring former Dead Kennedy and free-speech campaigner Jello Biafra. Unsurprisingly, his next move took him away from Warner Brothers.

Following their frontman to Priority Records, Body Count released their second album, *Born Dead*, subsequent to a punishing global tour calculated to gauge audience reaction. 'While the audience were watching us, we were watching the audience,' explained Ice-T. Although remaining a controversial figure (the rapper's activities were periodically monitored for subversiveness by the FBI) via the written and spoken word, the Ice's delayed 1993 solo rap album *Home Invasion*, like *Born Dead*, failed to raise much of a stink with lyrics like the anti-war 'Shallow Grave' – just as intense, but far less intrinsically controversial than 'Cop Killer'. Despite this, Ice-T remained undaunted: 'We would much rather have people say, "Yo! This is a good slammin' record."'

'Hardcore rap has run into a stonewall where it's hard to get the venues, 'cause the media's hyped it up into every time we have a concert someone gets killed, which is bullshit.' – Ice-T

Musically, the album represented more of a collective labour than the five-piece's previous effort – despite Ice-T retaining his position at the head of the table as lyricist. Guitarist Ernie C delineated the shift in direction: 'There wasn't so much of that "Cop Killer" stuff, and we didn't want people to think of it as an Ice-T side project . . . ' Citing the band's influences, C states, 'We are . . . increasingly influenced by the Hendrix idea of jamming, in a Megadeth and Slayer mode, but I also want to take things into a more loose, Zeppelin-orientated feel for the future. On the second LP we wrote the songs more as a band.' Despite this pluralist ethos *Born Dead* made little inroad upon the Top 100, hastening the departure of bassist Mooseman (who went on to work with Iggy Pop before his untimely death in a shooting incident).

Despite this comparative lack of success, Ice-T retained the project as a going concern and received encouraging reviews for the group's third album, *Violent Demise: Last Days*. But, though peppered with the Original Gangster's trademark tongue-in-cheek raps, sales once again proved disappointing, and the band has been mothballed while their frontman pursues his careers as a rapper and a movie actor.

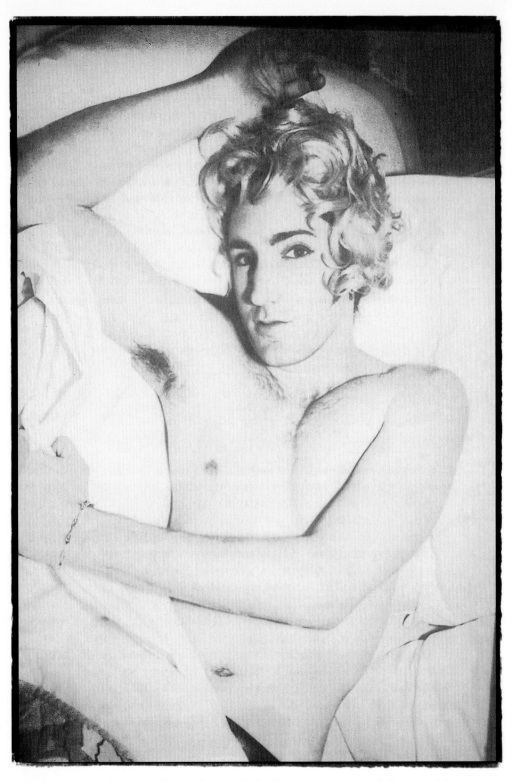

Trent Reznor's obsessions with sex and death, allied to his experimentation with electro-metal fusion, made him a favourite with both goths and industrial rockers.

I WANT TO FUCK YOU LIKE AN ANIMAL
Industrial/Alternative Metal

'I like technology. This is who I am.' – Trent Reznor, Nine Inch Nails

In 1994, after Kurt Cobain had made an exit, grunge was removed from the next season's schedules. Thousands of educated, white, middle-class rock fans packed away their lumberjack shirts for the final time, the 're-birth of rock' having become a wake.

More so than the New Wave of British Heavy Metal, grunge had grafted the punk aesthetic onto metal. An essentially American phenomenon based around a small number of bands – Nirvana, Pearl Jam, Soul Asylum, Mudhoney and Soundgarden – the genre reworked the early seventies guitar sound of Neil Young and Crazy Horse, or early Black Sabbath, while adopting the independent ideals synonymous with the US hardcore scene. The grunge sound was both melodic and distorted, the groups eschewing all visual theatrics to speak directly to the disaffected Generation X.

It was not until after the suicide of Cobain that the media spotlight fell on the diversifying 1990s metal and punk scenes. The Offspring, Green Day and Bad Religion were catapulted to chart success as part of the high-energy US punk scene, with roots in bubblegum hardcore bands like the Ramones. These bands employed a similar back-to-basics approach to grunge, albeit with more traditional rock 'n' roll lyrical content: unrequited passion, parental hassles and teenage angst.

> *'I don't have any answers. I just want to kick you in the ass and get you off your seat so that we can come up with the solutions together. Forget Ministry, forget all your little idols, rock stars you have on the wall. Listen to us, process it and spit it out. Think for your fucking self.'* Al Jourgensen

Elsewhere, Alain Jourgensen's Ministry and Trent Reznor's Nine Inch Nails were enjoying great success with a savage hybrid of metal and industrial electro merged

Ministry's Al Jourgensen and Paul Barker – the main creative force behind the band.

with gothic and hardcore aesthetics. Originally formed in 1980, Ministry had achieved little tangible success prior to Jourgensen's recruitment of partner-in-noise Paul Barker in 1988. (Up to that point, Ministry's frontman was best known for side projects the Revolting Cocks and Lard, with ex-Dead Kennedy Jello Biafra.)

The first Jourgensen-Barker Ministry recording, *The Land of Rape and Honey*, established the darkly aggressive, sample-soaked sonic assault that was to define the band. 'I still think it had lots of fucking attitude,' reflects Barker. 'For me it's kind of like listening to the first Public Image Ltd record. I feel like, "Wow this is so awesome! These guys are saying 'fuck you' to punk rockers." It's so bad ass.' Jourgensen had previously disassociated himself from Ministry's debut album, 1983's *With Sympathy*, describing it as 'an abortion' with style and content largely dictated by their record label, Arista. The follow-up, *Twitch*, was produced by On-U-Sounds dub production genius Adrian Sherwood and represented a massive improvement on the synth-pop of its predecessor. 'All major labels will try to see what they can get away with, and how much they can control you,' explains Jourgensen. 'We finally put our foot down with *The Land of Rape and Honey*, and since then, as long as the ground rules are set, they've pretty much left us alone.'

Ministry's fourth album, *The Mind is a Terrible Thing to Taste*, brought the band to national prominence, along with an extensive tour and subsequent live album, *In Case You Didn't Feel Like Showing Up*, described by the *LA Weekly* as 'the focal point of the true, new antisocialism'. Despite this acclaim, Jourgensen insisted the appeal of the band was limited: 'I don't see this music being accepted on a national level, if it does happen, it'll be disappointing . . . it means it's not threatening enough people.'

'I still think it had lots of fucking attitude, for me it's kind of like listening to the first Public Image Ltd record. I feel like, "Wow this is so awesome! These guys are saying 'fuck you' to punk rockers." It's so bad ass.' – Paul Barker on Ministry

The period between 1990 and 1992 represented a creative zenith for Jourgensen. The electro terrorist and polymath found time to record an EP under the name of 1,000 Homo DJ's featuring a cover of Black Sabbath's 'Supernaut', was in demand as a producer (most notably on Nine Inch Nails' 1990 cover of Queen's 'Get Down Make Love'), and featured in loosely-assembled collaborations such as Pailhead, Skrew, Acid Horse and the twisted country-and-western stylings of Buck Satan and the 666 Shooters. In 1991 Ministry recorded their seminal single 'Jesus Built My Hot Rod', featuring the manic redneck vocals of Butthole Surfer Gibby Haynes – a breakneck ride along a hardcore highway of techno rhythms and churning metal guitars. 'Hot Rod' was Ministry's biggest commercial success and gave Warners their highest selling single of 1991. Two more singles released the following year, 'NOW' and 'Just One Fix', resurfaced on the band's 1992 album *Psalm 69: The Way to Succeed and the Way to Suck Eggs*. A raging sonic behemoth of an album, *Psalm 69* was described by *Creem* as 'a new kind of heavy, as Wagnerian guitars swoop and fire like Kilgore's helicopters in *Apocalypse Now* . . . what teenagers dance to while the earth is being destroyed . . . ladies night in a slaughterhouse.' The album went platinum and established the band as pioneers of industrial metal. Jourgensen was characteristically dismissive of the hype, stating, 'I use industrial noises, but so what? I use whatever it takes to get the type of atmosphere I want on a song. I use guitars, that doesn't make me Led Zeppelin.' Despite this, Ministry are regularly cited by nu-metal bands such as Static-X as being hugely influential. Barker is ambivalent about such kudos: 'I don't pay attention to all that shit . . . That's another question we get all the time, like, "What do we think of these [nu-metal]

Sleeve art from Psalm 69: The Way to Succeed and the Way to Suck Eggs *(1992).*

bands?' I don't care. They know what they're doing. At least they have the balls to credit us . . . I like Static-X, I think they're funny.'

In 1993/94, Jourgensen relocated to 'Ranch Apocalypse' (named after the site where messianic preacher David Koresh and his disciples had recently died in an FBI raid), a self-built studio at a former whorehouse in Austin, Texas. There, the band began work on the *Filth Pig* album, which was slower, heavier and more melodic than previous Ministry recordings. 'It isn't too much of the "happy shiny people" side of life,' conceded Barker, 'but hell, is yours? It's really slow in parts, fat and ugly all around and perhaps, the most pure riff-driven Ministry album yet.' But sales were disappointing, and the band retreated back to the ranch. In the latter part of the 1990's, Ministry were dropped by Warner Brothers following disappointing sales on their seventh album, *Dark Side of the Spoon.* As the title suggests, Jourgensen has also endured personal problems connected to a series of arrests for possession of heroin and cocaine.

However, the band are regulars on the movie soundtrack scene – contributing the track 'Bad Blood' to *The Matrix* and working closely with Steven Spielberg on the blockbuster *A.I.* Integration into Hollywood has not blunted Jourgensen's cutting edge, however. 'I told Steven Spielberg, dude – there's been some mistake,' he describes their initial encounter. 'The band thought it was a porno, that *A.I.* was like *Anal Intruder* or something like that.' In the summer of 2001, Ministry released a retrospective album, *Greatest Fits*, that, along with the duo's cinematic endeavours, is part of a plan to reach new audiences – despite Jourgensen's former stated intent to 'threaten' audiences rather than entertain them – as is playing support spots for more commercially successful bands.

Former computer engineering and music student Trent Reznor began his musical career by working as a night janitor in a recording studio. Interested in the mechanics of record production, Reznor approached the studio manager to ask if he could use the equipment while nobody was there. The resulting experimentation gave birth to a demo, 'Down on It', that secured him a recording contract with the TVToons label (previously responsible for nothing more subversive than a series of TV soundtracks). Nine Inch Nails' first album, *Pretty Hate Machine*, was a tormented fusion of gothic angst with the industrial soundscapes previously explored by bands like Throbbing Gristle, Einsturzende Neubauten and Cabaret Voltaire. Eager to take his project on the road, the one-man-band recruited a group of musicians and joined the 1991 Lollapalooza tour. However, as Reznor explained, converting the technologically-complex studio sound into a stage set presented formidable obstacles: 'I didn't want to have three guys onstage, faking everything, with a tape machine running. However, I also didn't want a seven-piece rock band where every cool bit of electronics was converted into people approximating it live on other instruments . . . So we used four tracks of tape and four musicians: I'd play guitar on some songs and sing, plus a keyboard player, a guitar player and a drummer.' The 1992 release of the acclaimed *Broken* EP served to widen the band's fan base.

'I don't see this music being accepted on a national level, if it does happen, it'll be disappointing . . . it means it's not threatening enough people.' – Al Jourgensen

Trent Reznor is, like Al Jourgensen, something of a one-man music industry – in addition to Nine Inch Nails, he has established his own label, Nothing Records, managed and produced acts such as Marilyn Manson and British rap-greasers Pop Will Eat Itself, and produced the music-dialogue soundtrack album for Oliver Stone's *Natural Born Killers*. Hailed by legions of trenchcoat-wearing goths, winner of a Grammy for the song 'Wish', NIN (basically Reznor himself, by this point) disappeared into the studio to record a new album. *The Downward Spiral* was written, arranged performed and recorded in the Hollywood house where actress Sharon Tate was murdered by the Manson Family. Whatever vibes Reznor was hoping to assimilate from the locale certainly worked. A brooding miasma of fear and loathing, *The Downward Spiral* was a massive hit and quickly achieved platinum sales.

Reznor, a classically trained pianist, has eclectic tastes which take in such diverse acts as drum-and-bass pioneer Goldie and avant-garde industrial virtuoso

Richard James (the Aphex Twin). Very much at home with the technological aspects of record production, Reznor draws inspiration from rock, classical, experimental and jungle music, using a multitude of samples to create a new aural soundscape. The content of *The Downward Spiral* ranges from the jagged, metal guitars of 'Mr Self Destruct' through the twisted, 808-driven synth-pop of 'Closer' to the haunting piano and vocals of 'March of the Pigs'. 'This was a difficult album to make,' explains Reznor, 'I didn't really have a definite idea of how it should sound. I mean, I had a theme lyrically and vibe wise [disease, sex and pain], but musically I wanted to put more emphasis on textures and mood . . . I had to develop a whole new palette of sounds.'

Reznor's obsessive method of sampling is reminiscent of pioneering b-boys such as Double D and Steinski, as illustrated by his description of the painstaking process: 'My assistant, Chris Vrenna, probably went through 3,000 movies listening to them without watching. Not to find the cliché spoken dialogue sample, but

just to hear sounds. He'd go through them on DAT, then I'd listen to them – I didn't know where they came from – and I'd cut 'em up into little segments and process them further through Turbosynth, or whatever. We compiled almost ten optical disks of things like that. We'd do a new song: "Okay, what's the mood?" "It's grim." So we'd put up a bank, find a sound and set it aside.'

Five years separated *The Downward Spiral* and

Perfectionist Trent Reznor takes great pains to ensure Nine Inch Nails shows are not merely a live approximation of his electronic studio sound.

the 1999 release *The Fragile*, during which time Reznor issued an album of remixes (*Further Down the Spiral)* and received a Grammy nomination for 'The Perfect Drug', which appeared on the *Lost Highway* movie soundtrack. Reznor describes *The Fragile* as 'focused on taking an element of rhythm 'n' blues and funk – in the Prince sense, not the Red Hot Chili Peppers sense – and juxtaposing it radically with an Aphex Twin-ish approach. It has the feel of something you might understand, but the sound of a stereo exploding. With a nice melodic song on top.' Despite his often discomfiting material, Trent Reznor's contribution to blowing open the boundaries of modern music cannot be understated.

'We were just doing this fucked-up noisy shit, and Bon Jovi was king of the world.' – Rob Zombie

While Reznor and Jourgensen were employing sampling technology to extend the parameters of rock, Rob Zombie was employing samples within a more traditional metal framework. Born Robert Cummings, Zombie is the horror film and comic book-fixated rocker who formed White Zombie in 1985. Named after the 1932 Bela Lugosi film, White Zombie was initially comprised of Rob Zombie (vocals), his girlfriend Sean Yseult (bass), Tom Guay (guitar) and Ivan de Prum (drums). Throughout the decade the band went through a number of changes, with Zombie and Yseult remaining as guitarists as drummers came and went. Originally part of the New York noise scene created by acts like Lydia Lunch, Sonic Youth and Foetus, White Zombie soon eschewed the art-rock of the Lower East Side scene to splice classic metal aggression to samples lifted from old B-movies. Overlaid by Zombie's breathless redneck-rap vocals, the group fused elements of metal, punk, funk and reggae to create a sound described by their frontman as being like 'a picture of a big monster with his tongue hanging out, drooling and driving a car.'

A series of independent releases culminated with the band being signed by Geffen in 1990, the trio of Yseult, Zombie and de Prum joined by guitarist J for their album, *La Sexorcisto: Devil Music Vol. 1*, in 1991. Described by Zombie in exploitation-movie poster terms as 'Murder! Catfights! Kidnapping! Sexcitement explodes on the highway to the pulsating sounds of forbidden pleasures,' *La Sexorcisto* spawned the double platinum-selling single 'Thunder Kiss '65' – its belated success promoted by a video (featuring a memorable cameo from Iggy Pop) that featured on MTV's *Beavis and Butthead* almost a year after its initial release.

The tongue-in-cheek mock-horror theatrics of White Zombie and their larger-than-life frontman were welcome relief from the introspective navel-gazing of the grunge era. Marrying the deranged hillbilly image exploited by Les Claypool's innovative band Primus to a satanic-biker aesthetic, Rob Zombie is dismissive, as Al Jourgensen once was, of suggestions that the band could explode into the mainstream in a similar manner to Nirvana: 'That was pretty much a once in a lifetime success. It's great but I wanna be in a band that has a loyal, hardcore cult following that are into it for the right reasons. Not get plastered everywhere so everyone gets into you, and in six months they get so sick to death of you, they never want to hear your name again . . . I'd rather be like the Grateful Dead – large audience that never

Rob Zombie: the undsiputed king of automotive horror metal.

White Zombie at the height of their powers, Astro Creep: 2000 *(1993).*

dies – if that's possible.'

In 1993, White Zombie released their second album, *Astro-Creep 2000.* Like the Grammy-nominated *Thunder Kiss, Astro Creep* went on to sell in excess of two million units, remaining in the *Billboard* Top 200 for 89 weeks. The new album moved the band further into crossover territory, incorporating more samples, electronics and funk/rap influences than its predecessor – the Grammy-nominated single 'More Human than Human' being particularly representative, with a video born of Rob's pop-culture sensibilities featuring cool Japanese robots, horror-movie posters and various trash ephemera. Aware of numerous cases of litigation surrounding the use of samples, the band took the innovative step of actually recording their own *faux*-movie dialogue to avoid being sued. 'When people ask, "Where is that sample from?" – I'm just like, I don't know,' admits Zombie of his pre-emptive defensiveness. 'I'm not telling anyone because I don't want to be in court in a year being sued by fucking Leonard [Mr Spock] Nimoy.'

'I wanna be in a band that has a loyal, hardcore cult following that are into it for the right reasons.' – Rob Zombie

In terms of musical content, Zombie cites hardcore hip-hop as an inspiration. 'When I first heard Public Enemy, just this dense layering of stuff, it didn't sound like anything else, just this rhythmic raging noise,' he acclaims – though most of his influences are rock-orientated. He describes seminal black hardcore band Bad Brains as 'the coolest band on the planet', and also cites Alice Cooper, KISS, Black Flag and the Ramones among his favourites. Naturally, given his penchant for

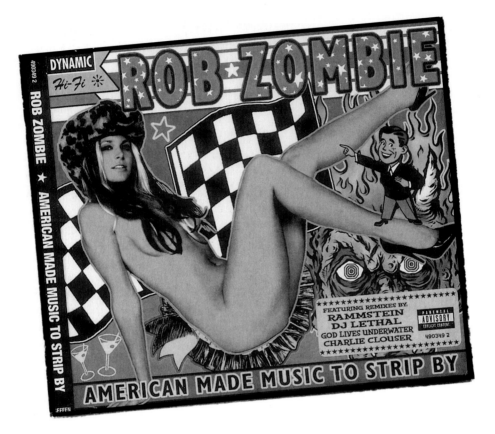

Rob Zombie's fascination with studio techniques gave rise to a remix of his Hellbilly Deluxe *album* – American Made Music To Strip By *(1999).*

satanic imagery, Zombie was a huge Black Sabbath fan: 'I would just look at the guys in Black Sabbath and think, "They look cool," and I would look at Led Zeppelin and go, "Those guys just look like hippies." The hippy thing always aggravated me, even as a kid. Sabbath were scary and dressed in black, and Zeppelin were wearing sandals and flowered, puffy shirts.'

After completing a world tour and releasing an album of remixes, *Supersexy Swingin' Sounds* – which featured production work by the Dust Brothers, PM Dawn and the Damage Twins, among others – Rob Zombie effectively allowed the band to drift apart. As well as branching out into movie soundtracks (including *Private Parts* and *The Crow*), artist management (with his brother Spider's band – Powerman 5000) and film direction (the upcoming *House of 10,000 Corpses*), Zombie recorded a solo album, *Hellbilly Deluxe,* released by Geffen in

*A talented illustrator in his own right, long-time comic book fan Rob
Zombie has hired noted artists such as Gene Colan and Daniel Brereton to
produce his album art.*

1998, followed by an album of remixes entitled *American Made Music to Strip By*
the following year. Zombie's solo material continues to feature the trademark hor-
rorshow samples and heavy riffing of his former band. In 1998, he recruited a new
backing band incorporating ex-White Zombie drummer Tempesta as well as former Nine Inch Nails guitarist Danny Lohner, the trio debuting as support on
Korn's Family Values tour.

Korn: David Silveria, Head, Fieldy, Munky, Jonathan Davis.

FAMILY ENTERTAINMENT
Korn

'You don't know me, but you don't like me. You say you care less how I feel. But how many of you that sit and judge me have ever walked the streets of Bakersfield?' – 'Streets of Bakersfield', Homer Joy

Korn released their eponymous debut album in 1994, defining the parameters of nu-metal. In addition to the obligatory fusion of hip-hop rhythms, rap and churning metal riffs, Korn added a heavier, more visceral element with their use of seven-string guitars and a five-string bass. Originally developed for use by jazz musicians, the extra bass strings gave the group a distinctively dense, resonant sound.

The band originated in Bakersfield, California, its townsfolk described by frontman Jonathan Davis as 'a lot of hicks. Crazy white-trash people.' The band's musicians – Brian 'Head' Welch (guitar), Reggie 'Fieldy' Arvizu (bass), David Silveria (drums) and James 'Munky' Schaffer (guitar) – moved from Bakersfield to Los Angeles and enjoyed minor success under the name LAPD. At this time, frontman Davis was emerging from a miserable adolescence and gigging with Bakersfield ensemble SexArt. Spotted by Munky and Head on a return trip to their hometown, Davis was approached to provide fresh vocal impetus for the quartet, by now in a creative impasse.

The new line-up bonded immediately. 'When we first got together, we felt the commitment. We knew this was right. We knew we were a team and the vibe was there,' recounts Davis. The origins of the name 'Korn' are shrouded in rumour – but the most credible explanation is that it was coined after the hilarious tale of a gay guy felching a fuck-buddy, who accidentally retrieves a piece of corn from his friend's arse with his tongue. The newly-christened Korn set about recording a four-track demo entitled *Niedermeyer's Mind,* produced by Ross Robinson. The demo – featuring the tracks 'Blind', 'Predictable', 'Daddy' and 'Alive' – immediately established a unique hybrid sound that owed more to the band's interpersonal chemistry than any contrived attempt at fusion. 'The sound just came out. We never tried to do anything special. Fieldy's into a lot of hip-hop, and me and Munky are into a lot of guitar shit like Mr Bungle and old Cypress Hill,' explains Head. 'We aren't a band that tried to mix hip-hop, industrial and metal, we're a blend of these sounds,' concurs Davis.

Lyrically, Davis strip-mined his childhood traumas and teen angst for inspiration. A sickly, asthmatic child, he was a fan of new-romantic pop band Duran Duran, and his adoption of their pretty-boy look let him in for a good deal of bullying at school. Without a trace of irony, Davis still pays homage to his youthful heroes: 'They were a bad-ass band. They conquered the world. I love that *Rio* album – that was the best one. *Arcadia.* I was off my rocker listening to that shit.' Labelled a 'faggot' by his peers and sexually abused by a neighbour, Davis was regularly left to his own devices by his musician father. Unhappy memories of this period, along with recollections of his tenure working as a mortician, provided the anguished subject matter for the band's first two albums and loaded the dark overtones of their sound with substance. As Davis said, 'Our sound is a combination of minor key, dark music with a groove and a hip-hop edge to it.'

'When we first got together, we felt the commitment. We knew this was right. We knew we were a team and the vibe was there.' – Jonathan Davis

Head and Munky's seven-string guitars gave Korn the heaviest sound around. It also sparked a revival of interest in a guitar model originally developed for manufacturers Ibanez by axe-virtuoso Steve Vai. While Head's preference for heavy, low-end grooves can be traced back to his admiration for George Clinton and Afrika Bambaataa, Munky had been introduced to the seven-string via Vai's savage and unrestrained *Passion and Warfare* album (1993). 'Fieldy got a five-string Ibanez bass when the band was getting started,' revealed Head, 'and he told Munky he should check out one of these seven-string guitars because it had a low "B". When I joined, I bought my first seven-string too, and we developed from there. The seven-string brings out heavy riffing. It's the Korn sound.' Munky himself described their use of the instruments in a round-table discussion for *Guitar World* with Vai and Incubus guitarist Mike Einziger: 'None of us in Korn have the technique that Steve has, but that doesn't prevent us from expressing ourselves in an interesting way. Instead of soloing in a traditional manner, we've learned to communicate by creating really raw and emotional sounds using new combinations of textures. I use a lot of different effects – uni-vibes, phasers and wahs, as well as fuzz boxes – but it's a matter of using the sounds in the right context and the right part of the song.' The effect of the seven-string is heightened by Munky

The sinister sleeve art from Korn's self-titled debut.

and Head's practice of tuning the guitar down one full octave, with the bottom string at 'A'. For his part, Vai was taken aback by the manner in which Korn utilised his brainchild: 'It's quite a sonic overload. One day I was coming from the zoo and heard Korn on the radio. I was stunned. It sounded like a herd of buffalo wearing iron shoes and blowing fire out of their nostrils.' Interplay between the twin guitarists is a key part of the Korn sound. 'We feed off of each other rhythmically a lot and work together', explained Munky. 'We play a lot of parts in unison, or I'll play a steady riff whilst Head plays counterpoint fills, like we do in the beginning of "Blind". But when it comes to big, fat choruses I'll break off and do a harmony or just play along with Head, only an octave higher or lower.'

'Before I got in Korn, I tried out to be Jesus Christ, just so I could face his ass.' – Jonathan Davis

Niedermeyer's Mind attracted the attention of Immortal Records (a subdivision of Epic) A&R man Paul Pontius. After experiencing the blistering power of the band live, Pontius signed the quartet and the pre-production work on *Korn* began immediately. Set numbers such as 'Blind' and 'Daddy' underwent drastic reconstruction, and the demo track 'Alive' was scrapped, with elements of the song incorporated into a new piece entitled 'Need To'. Intensive rehearsal at an Anaheim studio also yielded a new set of songs, including 'Ball Tongue', 'Clown', 'Helmet in the Bush' and 'Faget'. Davis recycled a more positive aspect of his childhood for public consumption by playing bagpipes (for which he won awards as a boy) on the sessions' stand-out track, 'Shoots and Ladders'. Keying into the malevolent undertones of nursery rhymes, the song exposes the intuitive meanings contained within the first songs many infants ever hear. 'Faget' (sic) concerned itself with Davis' experiences at the hands of high school bullies: 'Everyone thinks that I'm bashing gay people in this song and I'm not. It's really about me going through high school being called "pussy", "queer" and all that stuff, about getting picked on by all these jocks.' The album's final track, 'Daddy', ends with Davis sobbing into the mike, recounting his abuse at the hands of a neighbour and his father's disbelieving indifference. The intense effect of performing the song on Davis seems in no way contrived. Consquently, the band have only attempted to play 'Daddy' live on one occasion. 'I fucking had a lot of shit on my mind a long time that I wanted to get out,' Davis said of the catharsis of facing his childhood traumas, 'and our producer, Ross Robinson, brought it out from me.'

'One day I was coming from the zoo and heard Korn on the radio. I was stunned. It sounded like a herd of buffalo wearing iron shoes and blowing fire out of their nostrils.' – Steve Vai

Korn hit the stores on 4 October 1994 with no great fanfare or media interest. The band promoted the album by touring with Biohazard and House of Pain, the beginning of a two-year period that saw them establishing a fan base with their blisteringly intense live set (minus the problematic 'Daddy'). Building themselves up to a nightly fever pitch, the group played over 380 gigs in one 365-day period. This punishing schedule was largely fuelled by alcohol, although Davis developed a speed habit he claims 'kept me up for two years straight'. In addition to headlining their own shows, Korn opened for Ozzy Osbourne, Marilyn Manson, Megadeth, Cypress Hill, Fear Factory and Primus. Audience word of mouth negated the complete lack of airplay. By the end of 1996 *Korn* was selling at the rate of 17,000 albums a week. The band's reputation also spread to Europe, where the album was released over a year after it was made available in the US. Despite sold-out shows, however, the band found intercontinental touring a grind. 'It fuckin' sucks,' complained Davis. 'We had a bad fuckin' experience in Germany, where some fucker tried to throw us out of a restaurant 'cause we were fuckin' American. The only places that were cool were London and Manchester . . . And Amsterdam – Holland's cool. Other than that, it was really fucked up.' The relentless touring eventually came to a halt at the beginning of 1996, with an exhausted band returning home just as *Korn* went gold.

Sacramento foursome the Deftones often drew comparisons with Korn, based on guitarist Stephen Carpenter's use of the Ibanez seven-string and vocalist Chino Moreno's emotionally-laden vocals. Initially redolent of alternative funkabillies

The Deftones: Abe Cunningham, Chi Cheng, Chino Moreno, Frank Delgado, Stephen Carpenter.

Primus, who fused funk and metal within a deep-fried redneck framework, the 'tones had been appearing regularly at Sacto's premier alt-rock venue, the Cattle Club, since 1990. The band never released any independent product, preferring to wait until the Warner subsidiary Maverick signed them before releasing their debut album *Adrenaline* in 1995. Produced by Terry Date, who had previously overseen the output of Pantera and White Zombie, *Adrenaline* sold in excess of 500,000 copies.

The Deftones struck up a relationship with Korn, as their two paths continually crossed on the road. It also led to the 'tones supporting the Bakersfield boys on a series of dates throughout the mid-nineties. While tracks such as '7 Words' and 'Engine No. 9' contained the furious tuned-down assault commonly associated with Korn, the remainder of the album showed the Deftones placing far more emphasis on melody and harmonics than their supposed mentors. Date's polished production also gave *Adrenaline* a far cleaner texture than the bludgeoning miasma of *Korn* or *Life Is Peachy* – Carpenter's soaring riffs and Moreno's vocal diversity defining the Deftones sound, while Korn are driven by their fearsome rhythm section.

'You can't go anywhere unless you overstep boundaries.' – Stephen Carpenter

Influenced by such diverse bands as Depeche Mode, the Cure and Bad Brains, the quartet's development soon followed a very different course to that of the rap metal-based Korn. The Deftones' second album, *Around the Fur*, experimented further with the band's sound via the addition of a DJ, Frank Delgado. 'He's not doing what you'd expect from a DJ,' explained Moreno of how his new bandmate used the record decks to add sound segments, 'he's not scratching or playing voice samples, he adds a bit of ambience to the music.'

Indeed, the band actively distanced themselves from the rap-metal genre. 'I wouldn't call us hip-hop at all,' stated Moreno. 'I mean, hip-hop is a whole lifestyle. It's an image that's in everything related to it. I don't think there's any of that imagery in any of our music. Also, I wouldn't even consider anything I do [to be] rapping. It's just, like, rhythmic singing.' The content of Morello's lyrics are often obscure, the singer's wide range of vocal techniques delivering the emotional impact of the song. 'What's good about listening to a song and knowing exactly – to the word – what the singer is talking about?' asked bassist Chi Cheng, defending Morello's impressionistic style. 'It's like a good painting or a good book. I never ask Chino what something means, I want to know what it means to me.'

The Deftones' music continued to progress with their third album, *White Pony*, in 2000. Once again produced by Terry Date, the band moved further away from the bludgeoning rap-metal fury demonstrated on *Adrenaline* towards a melodic, considered approach that had more in common with introspective alternative metal acts such as Stabbing Westward and Maynard James Keenan's dull-but-worthy Tool.

> '*All my lyrics just pertain to me and what I feel. I don't do it just to shock people, do you know what I mean? If I tried to shock people, I'd be like Marilyn Manson, talking about Satan and stupid shit like that – that's shock value stuff. This is real stuff that's happened to me. That's all I know.*' Jonathan Davis

With *Korn* still selling well after eighteen months, pressure began to mount on the band to record a follow-up. The downside of their take-it-to-the-audience approach to promotion meant there had been no time to create any new material. 'When you're a little baby band, the first album's always good,' Davis confirmed the cliché of the 'difficult' second album, 'because you've had all your life to write these songs. But the second album – you come off the road and you've got to get this album done, and then you've got to get right back out on the road.'

The band entered a period of intensive rehearsals and Davis confined himself to a Hollywood hotel room to provide lyrics. Ironically entitled *Life Is Peachy,* the new album applied the established formula of teen angst projected over bass-heavy guitars and pounding rhythms. Once again, Davis revisited his troubled past for songs such as 'Good God', 'Kill You' and 'Mr Rogers' – recounting, respectively, his childhood bullying by his peers, his hatred of his stepmother, and his personal disgust at the inane values that children's television attempts to impress upon the young. The album's opening track, 'Twist', is a frantic assault of thunderous noise and gibberish, of which the only decipherable word is the song's title, providing hours of fun for the hardcore Korn kids who attempted to glean the meaning of Davis' random scat-singing. The link between the two groups was strengthened by 'Chi', named after Deftones bassist Chi Cheng, while vocalist Chino Moreno guested on 'Wicked'. 'Ass Itch' was Davis's response to the pressure of providing lyrics on demand: 'I hate writing shit.' Ultimately, however, the angst-ridden vocalist's efforts were worthwhile. Head was quoted as joking that he hoped 'Jonathan doesn't get help; we're screwed if he gets cured'.

Life Is Peachy was released on 15 October 1996, and entered the *Billboard* chart at number three. Its success propelled the band into the big league. However, Head contended that Korn's nature precluded any mass appeal: 'I don't think we will ever be mainstream. We have no control over if we get played or not. I don't listen to radio, so I don't have to deal with it. But we want to make heavy music more acceptable. We want other bands like the Deftones and Limp Bizkit to get more play. If we get played then maybe they'll start adding more and more and more . . . we just make music for ourselves. Whatever comes after that, cool. I think that if we can move our-

Korn's 'difficult' second album – Life Is Peachy *(1996).*

selves, we can move anybody.' But *Entertainment Weekly*'s David Grad was distinctly unmoved, describing the album as 'a 50 minute primal scream' in which 'profanity driven rants like the aptly titled "K@#%!" or "Kill You" undermine the band's compelling fusion of heavy riffs and hip-hop beats, leaving the impression that frontman Jonathan Davis is turning his well-publicised childhood traumas into a cheap marketing device.' For his part, Davis issued a strenuous rebuttal of Grad's withering put-down: 'I'm not putting my feelings out to make money at all. I'm putting my feelings out for myself and other people; if I get money, that just comes with it . . .'

The punishing promotional tour took in the USA, Europe and Australia, before the quintet headed out on the 1997 Lollapalooza tour. The relentless tour-album-tour cycle finally exacted its toll when Munky was hospitalised with viral meningitis in mid-July. In the meantime, Korn won the *Kerrang!* best album award for *Life Is Peachy*, and a further boost to group morale arrived in the shape of MTV's decision to give the single 'A.D.I.D.A.S.' mass exposure – its title formulated from the schoolyard acronym (All Day I Dream About Sex) and as a namecheck to the band's stagewear sponsors. Inevitably, this exposure gave rise to a legion of sportswear-bedecked 'Korn Kids' as well as boosting the sales of *Life Is Peachy*.

Korn's extensive periods on the road had given the band the opportunity to present new acts to the 'Korn Kids' in a support slot. One of these groups was Limp Bizkit, fronted by Fred Durst, who introduced himself to the band via his tattooing credentials. 'Fred told us he'd been tattooing for years, but it turned out it was, like, his third tattoo!' Davis recalls of Durst's self-promotion. 'He did a "Korn" tattoo on Head's back – and it looked like "Horn".' Despite this, the band took the fledgling Bizkit under their wing, even forwarding their demo to record companies, 'getting them [Limp Bizkit] phat,' as Davis describes, 'taking them on the road with us for as long as we did, and we were like, "Fuck, we should have signed them to our own label."' And so Elementree Records was formed – the label's initial signing being electro-rockers Orgy featuring guitarist Ryan Schuck, a fellow ex-member of Davis's former band SexArt.

In March 1998, the band's notoriety began to match their commercial success. The assistant principal of Michigan's Zeeland High School, one Gretchen Plewe, professed herself deeply offended by the use of profanity in the band's lyrics. 'Korn is indecent, vulgar, obscene, and intends to be insulting. It is no different than a person wearing a middle finger on their shirt,' she proclaimed, passing a rule forbidding students from wearing promotional clothing with the offensive band-name. An eighteen-year-old student, Eric Van Hoven, fell foul of Ms Plewe's prejudices and was summarily suspended. The inevitable media shit-storm ensued, with politicians and concerned parents leaping aboard the bandwagon. However, Korn were now able to employ their newfound financial muscle to resolve the situation. Subsequent to legal advice, the band issued a statement denouncing the assistant principal's moralising and issued the school authority with a cease-and-desist order preventing her from making any further defamatory comments. Not wishing to incur the wrath of Sony's lawyers, no more was heard from the Michigan schoolteacher. Just to rub salt into Ms Plewe's wounds, the band produced 500 Korn t-shirts reproducing the US Constitution's First Amendment (the right to free speech) with the caveat 'Except in Michigan' printed on the back. These were distributed to Zeeland students with assistance from the local radio station.

'The first album I was just screaming my head off. The second album was screaming with a little bit of singing. The third album is singing with a little bit of screaming.' – Jonathan Davis

Despite the platinum status of *Life Is Peachy*, the band considered the album something of a rushed effort. Free from the immediate pressures of touring and with a greatly increased budget, they booked into Hollywood's NRG recording studio to produce their third LP. 'Everything was starting to sound the same and we needed to change it,' Davis recalls. With this in mind, the services of Ross Robinson were dispensed with and former Guns 'N Roses producer Steve Thompson was brought in. Davis also conceded that it was time to look to areas other than his childhood for inspiration. 'I can't keep doing that – it's going to get stupid. I've got to keep doing new things,' he acknowledged. The band felt that the slew of copyists that emerged in their wake had heightened the need for progress. It was this dynamic that provided the new album's title: *Follow the*

Leader. And the high profile of the band encouraged artists such as Ice Cube and Pharcyde's Tre Hardson to record guest vocals. It had also been hoped that Cypress Hill's B-Real would appear on the track 'All in the Family' – however, various commitments led Korn to enlist Fred Durst as a late replacement for the rapper. Durst and Davis's verbal duel provided one of the album's high points, attacking one another in alternate verses. Durst's hilarious parody of Davis annunciating, 'Are you ready?!' (from 'Blind') displayed the less intense ethos of *Follow the Leader.* The hitherto unforeseen combination of Korn and comedy was compounded by the recruitment of comedian Cheech Marin for the album's 'hidden' bonus track, a cover of Cheech and Chong's 'Earache My Eye'. The song was originally written as the legendary pothead duo's satire on 1970s glam-metal, for their 1978 film *Up in Smoke.* With lyrics like, 'My momma doesn't like me 'cos I wear my sister's clothes/She found me in the bathroom with a pair of pantyhose,' it was certainly a departure from Korn's usual tortured milieu. (Most of the band switched instruments to record the track, with Fieldy assisting Cheech on vocals,

Featuring cover art by Spawn *creator Todd McFarlane,* Follow the Leader *firmly established the band in metal's major league.*

Davis moving to the drum stool, and drummer David Silveria taking the bass.)

Korn, however, were unprepared for the cleanliness of the initial mixes produced by Thompson. 'It sounded to foreign to us,' explained Davis. The band unanimously decided to replace Thompson with sound engineer Toby Wright (though Thompson's name still appears on the album's credits). After nine months and a cost of $500,000, the band pronounced themselves delighted with the finished product. Fieldy claimed the band's first two albums 'sounded like demos' in comparison. As well as having a more polished sound, *Follow the Leader* carried more of an overt hip-hop influence than its predecessors. 'I think that all our fans really like hip-hop,' observed Fieldy. 'We took the Pharcyde out to tour with us. The first tour we ever did was with House of Pain . . . The hip-hop thing has always been there in us. Those songs broke up the album in a good way, because we have these heavy songs and then we have the hip-hop heavy songs. To me, if you take the vocals out of those songs, they're the heaviest fucking three songs on the record, you know? I mean, "All in the Family" – that song is so heavy, but it gets thrown off by the rapping . . . We're not going to become rap – if Jon started rapping, we'd probably giggle our asses off.'

The inclusion of seminal NWA rapper Ice Cube on the track 'Children of the Korn' added weight to the album's hip-hop credentials, as well as affording the band the opportunity to work with one of their heroes. 'I fucking love him,' proclaimed Davis, 'I was so scared to sing with him because he's like the one guy in hip-hop I respect. I've kind of lost it for hip-hop now, but old school – I love that shit. Him in NWA, and then him sitting there singing with me; I was freaking the fuck out. Like, singing with your favourite artist ever.'

Another strand of progression on *Follow the Leader* was Davis's vocals: 'The first album I was just screaming my head off. I barely sang on that album, it was just scream, scream, scream. The second album was screaming with a little bit of singing. The third album is singing with a little bit of screaming. It's just fine tuning what I am, I guess. You need a few albums just to figure out where the fuck you're at.'

Described by *Addicted to Noise* as 'scary and disturbing and disgusting and delirious', *Follow the Leader* made musical progress without damaging the band's status as angst kings. Songs such as 'Dead Bodies Everywhere' and the harrowing 'Pretty' recount Davis's tenure in the County Coroner's Office, satisfying those fans with any morbid curiosity about his past. 'I get a lot of people that come up to me crying,' Davis revealed of his more disturbed fans, 'saying they wanted to commit suicide but my song gave them an outlet to get all their aggressions out.'

Despite the acknowledged influence of hip-hop, 1998's Family Values tour was designed to be a showcase of heavy acts so that 'we don't . . . have too much of a mix up,' explained Fieldy. 'You've got to keep it kind of the same vibe. Like,

Still speaking out for the young and dispossessed. Untouchables *(2002) is a powerful return to form.*

Lollapalooza was just too mixed up, man. Like Tricky and Ziggy Marley and then Korn and Tool. It just doesn't make sense. You want everybody to like every band.'

This more one-dimensional line-up still proved problematic. While Elementree signings Orgy and long-time associates Limp Bizkit were easily recruited, Korn's 'brothers' the Deftones refused to appear. The root of this surprising snub was their absolute refusal to take the stage ahead of Durst's ensemble. While Limp Bizkit seemed amenable to swapping billing with the 'tones, the Sacramento outfit held firm, sticking to the schedule of what Fieldy described as 'a bullshit tour that they're hating right now'.

The long-standing relationship between the two bands was repaired by Korn inviting the 'tones to headline on the second Family Values tour, that following year. More pluralist in its approach, the rap aspect of Korn's aesthetic was represented by Ice Cube. As a balance to Ice's straight-up hip-hop, initial attempts to sign up Rob Zombie floundered due to the horror-meister's elaborate stage show, with German industrialists Rammstein brought in as late replacements. Described by Davis as 'the new Ministry', the Family Values tour was Rammstein's first major American outing. Intense and uncompromising, without the upbeat rhythmic elements that characterise the rap-metal bands, the non-English speaking Rammstein were named after a German airfield disaster. Davis was excited to work with them, enthusing about 'a fuck who sets himself on fire' in the Germans' line-up.

Before setting out on the Family Values extravaganza, Korn undertook a lightning promotional tour of record shops – enhanced by guest appearances by Fred Durst, Ice Cube, and millionaire entrepreneur and comic-book artist Todd MacFarlane, who provided the album's graphics. Many of the signing sessions were complete roadblocks, and the forthcoming single 'Got the Life' was receiving intensive advance airplay, but the album was released to mixed reviews. While *Rolling Stone* was fulsome in its praise, both *Spin* and *Entertainment Weekly* remained lukewarm, variously describing it as 'therapy' and 'dumb fun'. All criticism was swept aside in an avalanche of album sales: *Follow the Leader* shifted a staggering 268,000 copies in the first week of its release and hit the *Billboard* chart at number one in late August 1998. Less than a month later, the Family Values bandwagon left town and proved an immediate success, grossing around $240,000 per show. No expense was spared, and each act had its own interchangeable set, the tour enhancing the reputation of Limp Bizkit and propelling both Orgy and Rammstein towards a mass Stateside audience. The tour ended with a gala performance in Fairfax, Virginia on 31 October. Featuring Korn made up as a 'hair-metal' band, Limp Bizkit as Elvis and Rammstein stark naked, the trek ended on a high note. Three days later, Korn set off on yet another headlining tour.

The end of the millennium saw Korn at the top of the newly constituted nu-metal heap. Former protégés Limp Bizkit were by now a platinum-selling success story, and emerging outfits like Kid Rock, the Bloodhound Gang and the Disturbed were following the path to mass exposure trailblazed by the Bakersfield boys. Media acceptance came in the form of an MTV award for best rock video ('Freak on a Leash') and the band's fourth album, *Issues*, was released. Produced by Brendan O'Brien, the album lent a further layer of relative refinement to the quintet's sound. This was interpreted by many hardcore fans as a 'watering-down', Korn's thunder being stolen by the far more aggressive and powerful Slipknot.

Issues may ultimately represent little more than an attempt to create a main-stream-friendly Korn. Whilst the band remains one of the biggest names in the genre, nu-metal has moved on and disappointing sales have led to a reassessment of their direction. The band's fifth album, *Untouchables,* was subject to near endless delays and production costs that spiralled past the $4 million mark. Although Fieldy describes the extended recording period in Arizona in terms of the band having 'pulled some Aerosmith shit', Davis insists that 'Getting this album done was a big accomplishment. We worked really fucking hard on it.' During this hiatus Korn were repeatedly forced to deny that drummer Silveria was leaving the band to pursue his developing career as a model, Jonathan Davis was required to undergo treatment for a growing asthma problem and bassist Fieldy was subjected to torrents of press derision upon the release of his ill-conceived solo rap album/cash cow *Fieldy's Dream.*

Despite such difficulties, *Untouchables* represented something of a return to former glories, with crisp production by former Marilyn Manson and Soundgarden engineer Michael Beirhorn and memorable tracks like 'Here to Stay' complimented by sell-out tours on both sides of the Atlantic.

CHAIRMAN OF THE BOARD
Limp Bizkit and Fred Durst

'I think we've successfully set a landmark for this type of music. Other bands have combined singing and heavy rock and rap, but no one's done it all to the extent where the rap is totally hip-hop credible, the heavy parts can move 100,000 people at a time in an arena, and the melodies can make the whole world sing.' – Fred Durst, Limp Bizkit

To many, Limp Bizkit represent the epitome of nu-metal. The band's overt fusion of phat beats, rapped/screamed vocals and tuned-down, extra-stringed guitars, combined with frontman Fred Durst's media omnipresence, have polarised the opinions of millions of metal heads. Enter 'Limp Bizkit' into any search engine and you will find more sites dedicated to dissing the Bizkits than those singing their praises. Likewise, a cursory examination of the *Kerrang!* or *Metal Hammer* letter pages will usually discover at least one letter castigating the quintet while elsewhere on the page an outraged fan defends his heroes. As perceived standard bearers of the movement, Limp Bizkit are the prime target for anyone with a distaste for nu-metal – much of the opprobrium taking the form of personal attacks on Durst. As an individual, there is little that's particularly offensive about the man or his image – apart, perhaps, from an ego the size of Jupiter. However, his elevation to corporate status – as vice president of the band's label, Interscope – has led many politically-aware metal fans to accuse Durst of being little more than a dollar-fixated company shill. Durst himself has done little to deflect these accusations, describing Limp Bizkit as 'part of a fad' and adopting a siege mentality that precludes speaking to the media. Like Linkin Park – regularly labelled as little more than a manufactured group – Limp Bizkit are an easy target

Fred Durst: rap-metal trailblazer, or corporate shill?

simply because they appeal to the younger section of the nu-metal audience.

Formed in 1994 by Durst and bass player Sam Rivers, the band's initial line-up was completed with the addition of Rivers' cousin, jazz drummer John Otto, and guitarist Wes Borland. Based in Jacksonville, Florida, the band derived their Led Zeppelin-style misspelled name from a stoned acquaintance of Durst's who claimed his fried grey matter felt like 'a limp biscuit'. The band started gigging at Jacksonville's Milk Bar, their fusion sound soon garnering them a small local following. The more traditionally-orientated local groups were less thrilled, later dismissed by Durst as 'totally stiff dorks with tight jeans, red-necking metal bands.' As detailed previously, Limp Bizkit's big break came via Durst's tattoo-parlour liaison with Korn's Fieldy and Head, subsequent to the Bakersfield boys' 1995 Jacksonville gig. A demo tape featuring the tracks 'Pollution', 'Stuck' and 'Counterfeit' was given to Fieldy, who then passed it on to producer Ross Robinson. Robinson was suitably impressed by the raw, Korn-esque sound of the demo, and copies of the tape began to circulate among record labels and tour promoters. This ultimately led to Limp Bizkit's inclusion on the high-profile 1996 Vans-sponsored Warped tour, and support slots with Faith No More, Primus and House of Pain.

The support slot on a 1995 tour with ersatz-'oirish' rappers House of Pain (then on their last legs) provided Bizkit with their final member, DJ Lethal. 'I was without a band, Limp Bizkit seemed to be really cool and I thought they'd need a DJ,' explained Lethal. 'I thought I'd give it a try; they liked the idea. It was great, we really worked together well and what can I say? I'm still with Limp Bizkit.' As well as providing the requisite scratches and samples, Lethal's talents were utilised as a counterpoint to Borland's eclectic seven-string guitar sound. Borland defined the dymanic between them: 'He's almost like another guitar player. I don't work well with other guitar players, but him being a DJ, he can do stuff that I can work well with.' With the definitive five-piece Bizkit line-up in place, and a set of songs road-tested through constant touring, the band entered the Indigo Ranch studio with producer Robinson to produce their debut album.

Three Dollar Bill Y'all$ was mixed by Andy Wallace, who had previously produced Nirvana's seminal *Nevermind,* and arrived in US stores in July 1997. The album featured thirteen tracks, three of which – the heavy, angst-ridden 'Nobody Loves Me', 'Clunk' and 'Leech' – bore all the Robinson production hallmarks of aural angst and mayhem and were, unsurprisingly, heavily derivative of Korn. 'I think they should all start calling us "The Band That Sounds Like Korn,"' remarked Durst. 'We just shrug it off because getting upset wouldn't really change anything, and what good would it do?' Certainly, the album spends much time in Korn territory, and 'Nobody Loves Me' features an anti-mom polemic reminiscent of the Jonathan Davis approach to lyric writing. However, despite the band's admission of being overawed by their first experience of recording, *Three Dollar Bill* is more than another Ross Robinson nu-metal project. The eclectic guitar sound of Borland, alternating between thunderous riffing and a liquid jazz feel, established the musical direction that developed over Limp Bizkit's next two albums. The debut was a solid first attempt, with only two filler tracks: 'Indigo Flow', musical equivalent of a 'thanx' section in an album's sleeve notes, and 'Everything', sixteen long minutes of self-indulgent noodling possibly explained by Durst's admiration for nu-prog rockers Tool. Inevitably, it was the album's first single – a cover of George Michael's 'Faith' – that garnered the most attention and propelled the band on to MTV. Released at the time of Michael's arrest on indecency charges, it could, perhaps, be read as an indication of Durst's commercial cynicism. 'I liked it because I like George Michael,' he insisted. 'I always have. I always thought that was kind of a cheesy song. Everything he wrote was a hit and huge. I thought he was awesome, he was the mack.' Their leader's dubious musical tastes notwithstanding, Limp Bizkit's rendition of 'Faith' built to a level of intensity more commonly associated with Slipknot. While the album had initially sold slowly, the mass exposure of the 'Faith' video (an on-the-road homage to the Family Values tour) propelled *Three Dollar Bill* towards platinum sales.

> 'I like George Michael, I always have . . . Everything he wrote was a hit and huge. I thought he was awesome, he was the mack.' – Fred Durst

Galvanised by the success of their debut album, Limp Bizkit headlined their own tour during the early part of 1998. Supported by Clutch and Sevendust, the Ladies Night in Cambodia tour was a solid success – its name derived from the publicity-grabbing ploy of giving free entry to the first 200 female fans to turn up for their own ladies' night in a supposed 'war zone'. However, the band were soon to receive more unwelcome publicity. Reports in both the *Los Angeles* and *New York Times* exposed the band as unwitting beneficiaries of a cash-for-airplay deal between the Flip/Interscope label and the Portland, Oregon radio station KUFO-FM, allegedly at the latter's instigation – the track 'Counterfeit' being played 50 times over a period of five weeks. Durst was quick to play down the situation, arguing, 'This isn't payola – that's fraud and that's bullshit.' Regardless of such sharp practice, 'Counterfeit' remained on the station's playlist even after the deal had expired.

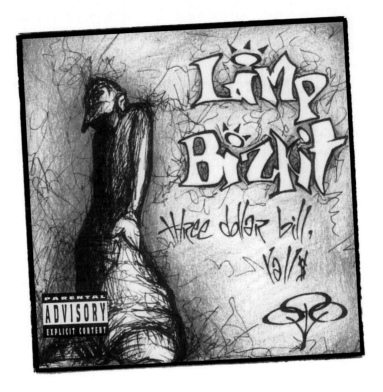

Limp Bizkit's debut album: Three Dollar Bill Y'all$ *(1997).*

The remainder of the year saw the band hop aboard the Warped, Ozzfest and Family Values roadshows, missing few opportunities to grab some column inches. Limp Bizkit's live show featured such setpieces as the band emerging from a giant toilet bowl, and from within a George Clinton-inspired Mothership, as well as break-dancers and VIP passes for female fans prepared to wave their tits before the hormonally-supercharged throng. This type of unreconstructed macho-jock behaviour drew criticism from the politically correct – *Spin* magazine's Chuck Eddy described the Bizkit audience as 'plenty of dudes in baggy shorts looking for reasons to kick teeth in'.

After an epic year of touring, Limp Bizkit headed straight to north Hollywood's NRG studios to begin work on their second album. *Significant Other* was released in June 1999, promoted by a series of carefully-orchestrated 'impromptu' live shows at locations such as the rooftop of the Chicago TRAX

Released during the summer of 1999, Significant Other
was Limp Bizkit's breakthrough album.

recording studio. Naturally, in order to gain maximum publicity, it was essential that these unauthorised public performances be brought to a premature end by the local police department. Dutifully, the cops played their part and brought the Chicago, Detroit and Boston shows to an early finish, amid a flurry of bogus posturing, with band and police playing out their respective pantomime roles.

Despite the manufactured outrage, Durst was keen to add more substance to the band's sound and recruited Stone Temple Pilots' frontman Scott Weiland as a voice coach. Explaining his curious choice of vocal trainer to MTV, Durst opined, 'I'd rather have one that's someone that I really loved and bought his records myself instead of some fat little gay guy' – though it's unclear whether this was just a cynical ploy to provoke outrage among overweight, diminutive gays.

Whereas *Three Dollar Bill* established the basis of the Limp Bizkit sound, *Significant Other* crystallised the group's unique fusion. Sporadically brilliant, the

'Everybody in the place now' – Fred Durst meets his public.

album gets off to a blistering start with its three most outstanding tracks: 'Just like This', 'Nookie' and 'Break Stuff'. After such a furious opening, the remainder of the album is largely mediocre – though Terry Date's high-definition production and the band's musical progression at least make for a recording that sounds nothing like Korn. 'Nobody can claim anymore that we sound like Korn,' declared Durst, cock-a-hoop to escape the pigeonhole, 'but there will be a lot of bands out there who want to sound like Limp Bizkit.' Produced by Gang Starr's DJ Premier, the track 'N 2 Gether Now' is the album's strongest elment of rap-metal fusion, teaming the Bizkits with the Wu-Tang Clan's Method Man to create a compelling mixture of laid-back hip-hop and nu-metal. (The video, featuring Durst and Method Man indulging in high-flying kung fu antics, became a staple on MTV.)

> 'I am a renaissance man, I'm trying to build an empire, leave a credible legacy.' – Fred Durst

Significant Other proved to be a massive commercial success, selling 634,874 copies in the first week of release and entering the *Billboard* chart at number one. The album went on to achieve multi-platinum sales and catapulted Limp Bizkit toward superstar status. However, this enormous success was tarnished as soon as the band headed out on the road. Following events at a 12 July show in St. Paul, Minnesota, Durst was charged with disorderly conduct and fifth-degree assault upon security guard Pat Estes. Durst claimed to have mistaken Estes for a 'rowdy concertgoer', while witnesses reported that Durst bragged after the event that he had 'kicked that punk-ass security guard in the head'. Despite the gravity of these charges (Durst potentially faced 90 days in jail, although the charges were later dropped), this fracas paled in comparison with the farrago of greed and violence at Woodstock '99. Originally envisaged as a means to cash in on the 1969 hippiefest, the 1999 version of Woodstock had more to do with fleecing a captive audience for every last cent than any legacy of peace and love. With prices for food and water hiked up to insane levels, poor stewarding and inadequate toilet facilities, the patience of the huge crowd was sorely tested. As the festival wore on their mood deteriorated, the organisers' response of sending a few old hippies out to mouth dated platitudes failing to bore the crowd into submission. The enthusiastic response to Limp Bizkit's set escalated into violence, and at least one sexual assault was alleged to have taken place while the group were on stage. Horrified by the reaction of the crowd, the organisers cut the power to the main stage and Limp Bizkit were forced to end their set ahead of time. The following day saw concession stalls tipped over and set alight, as well as some rioting. Rather than admit that penning an audience into a hot open-air arena and charging them six dollars for a small bottle of water was in any way provocative, the organisers identified Limp Bizkit's 'Break Stuff' as the catalyst of disorder. 'People try to pin a bunch of shit on us, like the Woodstock thing burning,' complained Durst of being raked over the coals by the the media, 'it is the greedy people that put it on treating people like cattle.'

'Nobody can claim anymore that we sound like Korn, but there will be a lot of bands out there who want to sound like Limp Bizkit.' – Fred Durst

Limp Bizkit saw out 1999 by headlining the Family Values tour, while their frontman juggled with his newfound corporate position of Interscope vice president – given in gratitude for shifting units. In addition to signing wearisome nu-grungers Staind and producing Jacksonville band Cold's second album of Pearl Jam pastiches, Durst found time to write a screenplay, direct the video for 'Nookie' and guest on albums by Korn, Videodrome and Soulfly. 'I am a renaissance man,' he claimed with typical modesty. 'I'm trying to build an empire, leave a credible legacy. Everything I do I want it to be better than the last time I was at bat. No room for failure, my attention span is too short for just one thing.'

The band began the new millennium with the release of their third album, *Chocolate Starfish and the Hot Dog Flavoured Water*. A slightly heavier recording than *Significant Other*, *Starfish* included the single 'Take a Look Around', which featured on the *Mission Impossible 2* soundtrack. The already high profile of the band was taken to a new plateau by the cinematic video for the single – a reworking of the *Mission Impossible* TV theme tune, 'Take a Look Around' explodes into a high-octane chorus that manages to be both catchy and mosh-worthy. *Chocolate Starfish* smashed previous sales records for rock albums, selling in excess of a million copies within a week of its October 2000 release. Produced by Terry Date with assistance from Josh Abraham, DJ Lethal and Swizz Beatz, the album featured an entire ensemble of guest vocalists drawn almost entirely from the hip-hop world: DMX, Redman and Xzibit joining forces with former New Kid on the Block Mark Wahlberg and Scott Weiland. Keen as ever to stir up some valuable controversy, Durst directed his lyrical ire upon the likes of Eminem, Trent Reznor and Christina Aguilera. The self-styled 'renaissance man' also missed few opportunities to criticise Slipknot, who he apparently feels threatened by, claiming the band were shit and their fans morons. The masked metallists responded in kind, threatening to kick the asses of Durst and his band (with the exception of Borland, who seems to have earned a grudging respect).

Two further singles were released from *Starfish*: 'Rollin'' – a poor man's rip-off of Kid Rock's 'Bawitdaba' – and the truly awful 'My Way'. But both were massive hits, and the Bizkits headed out on a world tour to promote both the album and Fred Durst Ltd. Durst's criticisms of the super-heavy sound of Slipknot may well have been a reaction to criticism that Limp Bizkit have strayed from their metal roots and become a pop act. Recently, Durst has announced that the fourth Bizkit album will be 'the complete opposite of *Starfish*', promising a much heavier sound. These preparations were thrown into disarray by the sudden departure of guitarist Wes Borland in October 2001. Immediately before Borland's decampment, Durst had identified him as the driving force behind this shift in emphasis: 'The new stuff Wes is sending me is really heavy. He's definitely thinking about some of the things that are bothering him, because it's a vulgar display of power.' Borland may have a modicum of bitterness to work out of his system, following widespread criticism of the album recorded with his side project, Big Dumb Face. Eclectic and self-indulgent, *Duke Lion Fights the Terror!!* is a patchwork quilt of styles and ideas that was universally ridiculed by reviewers and sank without trace. Upon his departure, Borland wasted no time in starting work with a new band, Eat the Day, alongside fellow former Big Dumb Face members Greg Isabel and Kyle Weeks.

In May 2001, Durst had launched his own record label, Flawless, at Amsterdam's Supper Club. With a roster initially comprised of Big Dumb Face, solo artist Kenna and yet another grunge revivalist combo, Puddle of Mudd, Durst has confidently proclaimed, 'These bands will last forever.' But his most immediate challenge was to find a replacement for Borland. While many would find the prospect of replacing Limp Bizkit's most talented musician daunting, Durst remains optimistic: 'The first thing that's gonna happen is we're gonna comb the globe in search of the illest guitar player known to man. Then . . . we're gonna finish writing the sickest new undeniable Limp Bizkit album you could ever imagine.' In the interim, the band have scheduled an album of remixes by the likes of Timbaland and William Orbit, entitled *New Old Songs*. Both Limp Bizkit and Fred Durst remain something of an anomaly – massively successful in terms of sales but routinely castigated in the rock press. Such criticism has little impact on a man whose values were succinctly revealed by his response to the question of what his fans meant to him: 'My livelihood. I mean, it's obvious.'

STRAIGHT OUT THE TRAILER
Kid Rock

'I can pick up a guitar and play a Hank Williams song, then I'll pick up the turntables and rock a basement apart. I can get on the drums and bust beats. And I can put it all together in the studio. You know my motto, man: If it looks good, you'll see it. If it sounds good, you'll hear it. If it's marketed right, you'll buy it. But if it's real, you'll feel it.' – Kid Rock

Kid Rock is the living embodiment of the fusion between rap and rock. Part rock caricature, part gangsta pimp, the self-proclaimed 'Bullgod' is nu-metal's premier showman – proving a white rapper does not have to induce the sort of cringing embarrassment associated with Vanilla Ice, and, perhaps most radically, that country music can be assimilated into the multicultural musical mix. Like his close friend and white-rap contemporary Eminem, Kid Rock's brash, egocentric persona gives rise to accusations of 'style over substance' from his critics. However, the Kid is a talented multi-instrumentalist who has paid his dues during what he describes as 'a ten year overnight success'.

Given that Kid Rock seems to have been around forever, it's surprising to learn that he's only in his early thirties. Born Robert James Ritchie on 17 January 1972, the Kid grew up in the white middle-class suburb of Romeo, Michigan, 40 miles from Detroit. The third of four children, young Robert was a precocious child and was often to be found performing shit-kickin' standards such as Jim Croce's 'Bad, Bad Leroy Brown' at parties thrown by his parents. Although weaned on seventies white rock acts like Bob Seger and Ted Nugent, Ritchie developed a taste for black music that didn't always meet with the approval of his siblings, as he recalls: 'Michael Jackson came on TV and I could fuckin' moon-

The Stone Cold Pimp of a Nation – Kid Rock.

walk! I could do all that gay shit and I could do it well. My brother smacked me in the head and said, "What are you doin'? Why aren't you fuckin' runnin' with the devil? Van Halen, motherfucker!"' Exposure to old-school rap icons like Whodini and Run DMC only served to lead Ritchie further from the approved norm. Before long, he began hanging out at the local Mount Clemens housing projects, joining a breakdance crew and establishing a reputation as a talented DJ. This behaviour proved incomprehensible to Ritchie's parents, a churchgoing Catholic couple with little experience of pluralist culture. In an interview with *Kronick* online magazine, Kid Rock described their horror at his lifestyle choices: 'My parents used to ask me all the time, "Why the fuck you goin' down to DJ parties for them niggers?" Flat out! They'd say shit like, "You can go DJ a wedding and make $300, but you'd rather run down there with them niggers and play for $50 and drink 40's [bottled malt liquor] all night." And they weren't that hardcore about us. I don't wanna make 'em out to be big racial people. It wasn't that bad. It was more like I was truckin' outta there to go on some pipe-dream to do somethin' I loved and they couldn't understand.'

'A lot of people told me that I'm committing musical suicide with my sound. They believed you can't mix rock, country and rap, and that crossover is dead. I always knew it would work. And it will always work as long as you're really into it and like what you're doing.' – Kid Rock

It was while pursuing this 'pipe-dream' by performing at local basement parties that Ritchie gained his stage-name from a random remark – 'watch that white kid rock!' 'I went to every fucking rap show from '84 on,' recalls Kid Rock, who at other times presents himself as little more than a trailer-park redneck. 'I still have all my ticket stubs. I've been supporting this shit from day one.' In answer to why the music of urban black America should influence a white boy from the middle-class suburbs of Detroit, Rock explains, 'It's total rock and roll. Chicks and limos and money and hanging out and fuck you, I don't want to go to school. That's what kids want to hear. It's what you want to hear when you're fifteen. It's the attitude.'

In 1988, having established a local reputation, the newly christened Kid Rock received his first major break when his demo tape attracted the attention of Boogie Down Productions. While he wasn't offered a record deal, the Kid was given the opportunity to open for Boogie Down Productions on tour. After eighteen months of performing and honing his rhymes, the Troop-suited, flat-topped

DJ/rapper was picked up by Jive Records to record his first album. *Grits Sandwiches for Breakfast* (1990) was co-produced by Kid Rock with West Coast rapper Too $hort and BDP's D-Nice. More hip-hop-orientated than Rock's later output, it was largely inspired by the boastful, innuendo-laden 'slack' rapping of 2 Live Crew and Blowfly. While *Grits* failed to make any impact in terms of sales, the record received a degree of notoriety when Washington State University's radio station, WSUC-FM, was hit by a $23,750 fine from the Federal Communications Commission for airing 'obscene, indecent, or profane language' in the form of Kid Rock's 'Yodelling in the Valley'. A tribute to the joys of cunnilingus, the song revealed a preoccupation with oral sex that would attract a degree of hostility on tour with Ice Cube. 'When I came on stage with my finger in the air and I said, "How many people in here like licking pussy?" Everybody kinda went, "Argh!" Bottom line is black guys front like they don't lick pussy, knowin' they do. I mean if you make love, you gotta lick pussy. How can you front that you don't do that? It makes you look like such an asshole. But the fact still remains – you come on stage in front of six or seven thousand black people and say, "How many people here lick pussy?" Let me tell you how many hands you're gonna get – Zero! I did it in twenty cities.' Cultural and sexual differences notwithstanding, Rock established an underground following and was soon able to relocate to New York on the basis of a $5000 advance from Jive. But relocation proved an unqualified disaster – the Kid's nearest brush with the big time was an encounter with Christopher (Superman) Reeve, while working as a car valet once the Jive money had run out.

'There's a place for hard rock, but it doesn't have to be an anorexic, spandex wearing, stupid, poofy haired jerk hopping around like a bunny on stage. It can be real, it can be down, without being stupid.' – Kid Rock

Following this career nadir, Rock was rescued from obscurity by Continuum Records who financed the recording of his second album, *The Polyfuze Method*. Released in 1993, the album was still chock-full of risqué material such as 'Blow Me', 'Fuck U Blind' and 'Balls in Your Mouth', a track that extensively sampled the radio rants of the once-controversial 'shock-jock' Howard Stern. However, *The Polyfuze Method* was a manifesto of musical fusion that incorporated such diverse elements as rock balladry, rapping, and the use of eclectic samples like the Doors' 'Soul Kitchen'. 'My sampler is my instrument,' explained Rock, 'Sure, I can go grab a Diana Ross record, fuckin' loop it up myself, and it's going to be a hit. All I gotta do is talk some shit over it. Which isn't easy, but a lot of people do that. But take that Diana Ross song, and put it together with an Ike Turner song and then throw original guitar over it and some beats behind it, and out comes a new thing.' The *Village Voice* gave the LP an enthusiastic review, describing Kid as 'a born rapper' and commending him for 'joining rap and metal with love for both and reverence for neither'. *Polyfuze* sold a little better than its predecessor and served to broaden Rock's cult following. The album was followed by a slice of pure cock-rock in the *Fire It Up* EP, featuring an early version of Rock's 1998 hit 'I Am the Bullgod'. *Fire It Up* was under-promoted by Continuum, with a very low number of copies pressed. It led to the inevitable split, and Kid returned to Detroit to found his own label, Top Dog. (This return to home territory also led to fatherhood, following the Kid's reconciliation with former girlfriend Kelly Russell.)

'It's total rock and roll. Chicks and limos and money and hanging out and fuck you, I don't want to go to school. That's what kids want to hear. It's what you want to hear when you're fifteen. It's the attitude.' – Kid Rock

During 1994-95, Rock also established links with Detroit's burgeoning rap-metal scene, headlining a series of gigs supported by Insane Clown Posse, Esham and Natas. Reflecting on this period, the Kid recalls, 'The Clowns are a couple of kids from around the area. Kinda dirty, ugly lookin' kids that really wanted to work hard to do somethin', so I thought I'd help 'em out. They even paid me some money to rap on one of their songs. I looked at it like I was helpin' 'em out. It was kinda stupid. I don't dig their music, I don't dig what they're talking about and I can't feel it – it's not real. Slim Shady is cool though.' Kid Rock had formed a friendship with another young Detroit rapper, Marshall Mathers – aka Eminem, aka Slim Shady – with whom he performed at a number of local venues.

Featuring guest appearances from Black Crowes keyboard player Eddie Harsch and soul vocalist Thornetta Davis, Kid Rock's third album, *Early Mornin' Stoned Pimp*, was released by Top Dog in 1996. Self-produced and distributed, it explored similar territory to *Polyfuze*, blending metal and rap with laid back mid-western rock. *Stoned Pimp* also provided the Kid with a degree of financial security, enabling him to buy his own home when his relationship with Kelly Russell disintegrated, and both parties entered a custody battle over their infant son. 'I sold, like, 14,000 copies straight out of my basement,' Rock recalls the first glimmerings of success. 'I took an $8,500 loan and flipped it into 120 grand in eight months. Now I got the

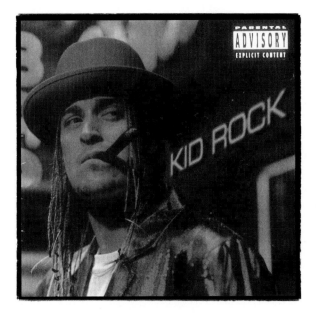

Devil without a Cause
*(1998) – nine million sold,
and still counting . . .*

bank calling me every day: "Would you like to invest some of your money?" I bought my own house. I bought a car. I got full custody of my kid. I'm doing real fine.' Such domestic responsibility was somewhat at odds with the image of the self-proclaimed 'pimp of the nation'. However, Rock juggled the dual roles of devoted single parent and hard-rocking chemical disposal unit with aplomb. Available to attend parent/teacher evenings as well as to chase 'ho's', Rock describes the schizoid nature of his existence: 'Snort lines all night and then drink 40's? Yeah, I do that! But that's on the road . . . I'm allotted to do that. When I'm home, it's up at 8.30. Put my kid in the bathtub; get him his waffles he's bitchin' about. Then he wants to play a couple of games of Nintendo, take him to school. Handle my business while he's at school, go to the park, work on music, make some phone calls. Fix some dinner for him, you know? Sit down, maybe go outside and ride the bike around or somethin'. Then stay up 'til 11.00 workin' on music, and go to bed.'

The buzz surrounding *Early Mornin' Stoned Pimp* – and Kid Rock's ability to sell out 5,000-capacity auditoriums in his home state – soon attracted major record company interest. 'I did a show and invited every label in the book,' the Kid recalled pimping for a corporate deal, 'nobody showed up but Atlantic. All of a sudden [A&R man Jason] Flom puts in a bid and three or four other labels came in and threw in a bid too. But the bottom line is that they got it because they were the first.' On signature of his first major contract, Kid Rock put together a backing band christened Twisted Brown Trucker – comprised of guitarists Jason Krause and Kenny Olson, Jimmy Bones on keyboards and Stefanie Eulinberg on drums. The line-up was enhanced by two backing vocalists, Misty Love and Shirley Hayden, as well as two performers who were to become integral to Rock's live show – a DJ, Uncle Kracker, and the childlike midget rapper Joe C. The ensemble then recorded

Released in the aftermath of the phenomenal success of Devil, The History
of Rock *mixed new material with highlights of the Bullgod's previous albums.*

what was to become the biggest selling rap-metal album to date – 1998's *Devil with-out a Cause*. The album's opening track, 'Bawitdaba', was a blisteringly-infectious hybrid worthy of comparison with anything produced by Run DMC or the Beastie Boys. When the video grabbed the attention of MTV schedulers the single became a massive hit, the exposure propelling *Devil* towards phenomenal sales that earned Rock a total of nine platinum discs. The remainder of the album demonstrated the versatility of the Kid and the Southern-fried sound of his neophyte backing band – ranging from the incongruous power ballad 'Only God Knows Why', and the funk of 'I Got One for Ya', to the MC5 metal-sampling of 'Somebody's Gotta Feel This' and the guest appearance of Detroit homie Eminem on 'Fuck Off'. 'Black Chick, White Guy', while supposedly demonstrating the softer side of Rock's nature ('Write about how sentimental I am,' he told an interviewer, 'I'll get more chicks'), describes the narrator's tempestuous relationship with a 'slut' he claims gave birth to

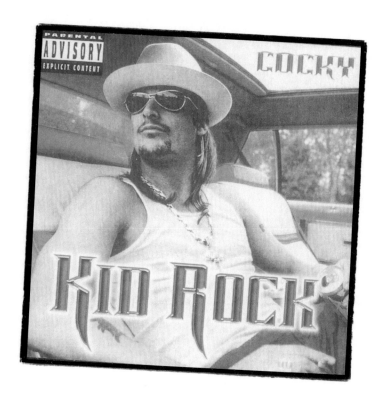

The Kid in full-pimp rock effect, for the sleeve of his 2001 album Cocky.

three children by different fathers when she 'didn't even know who the father was'.

The success of *Devil without a Cause* made Kid Rock the first white rapper to gain national exposure since Vanilla Ice, with his laughable imitation of MC Hammer. The Kid's take on Ice was, 'that fucker embarrassed, like, a whole generation of white kids,' while his views on current-day white rap were less apologetic: 'When I say, "Devil without a cause, white boy don't give a fuck," I'm rocking for the white kids. There may be some black kids that might feel alienated over it, but I mean no disrespect . . . It ain't got shit to do with colour. I don't live my life like that. But I love my honkies.' As for the content of the album, 'It's just about being true to yourself, being who you are . . . Don't be ashamed to grow up with money and enjoy rap music. Don't feel like you have to be a part of the ghetto to enjoy rap music. Don't feel that you can't be from the ghetto and like rock music. But that's the way it is right now and I'm one of the first people to come out in a long time and say "fuck that". You'll hear country, rap, fucking everything on there and you'll hear it done pretty fucking good.'

Throughout 1999, the Kid Rock roadshow brought its combination of metal, rap, country, midgets, explosions and strippers to the masses. As well as visiting Europe for the first time, Rock announced that the tour was to visit some of the customarily-overlooked destinations throughout the USA. 'Fuck playing New York City and LA, man', he dismissed. 'They can fucking have those places to themselves. I want to go to Iowa, I want to go to Indiana. Because those kids are ready, man. They want to party. They're not overexposed.' As sales of *Devil* continued to climb, work was begun on an album of remixes and re-recorded highlights from the Kid's first three albums. *The History of Rock* was released early in 2000, featuring two new tracks – the smash-hit single 'American Bad Ass' and 'Fuck That' – plus a number of previously unreleased demos. One of these, the overblown and satirical 'Abortion', received unwanted praise from the ultra-conservative 'pro-life' lobby – its final, country-pastiche stanza, where Rock sings about 'The second coming of Christ / It's God Himself in a jar,' somehow not dropping them the hint.

'Don't be ashamed to grow up with money and enjoy rap music. Don't feel like you have to be a part of the ghetto to enjoy rap music. Don't feel that you can't be from the ghetto and like rock music.' – Kid Rock

The History of Rock proved another solid commercial success, introducing those who had bought *Devil* to the highlights of the Bullgod's back catalogue. Any feelings of triumphalism were tempered, however, by the death of the Kid's friend, rapper Joe Calleja (Joe C) on 16 November 2000. The diminutive rapper, who was often mistaken for a child (most notably by a zealous photographic developer who reported pictures of Joe and some topless models to the vice squad), had suffered from an intestinal disorder, Celial disease, which required him to undergo extensive dialysis treatment and medication. The 26-year-old rapper had been forced to withdraw from Kid Rock's 1999 tour due to illness, but returned to the band for a series of dates with Metallica, System of a Down and Korn. As well as his work with Kid Rock and Twisted Brown Trucker, Joe C also recorded 'Kyle's Mom's a Big Fat Bitch' for the *South Park: Bigger, Longer and Uncut* soundtrack. 'For such a little guy,' Korn's Jonathan Davis paid tribute, 'he really lived big and walked big, and he's going to be missed.'

While the Kid's DJ, Kracker, enjoyed a slow-burning success with his million-selling *Double Wide* album, 2001 saw Kid Rock hit a peak of productivity. 'I've been cutting so much great stuff that I finished one [album] and just started another one,' he told *Kerrang!*. 'I'm going to put them out one at a time because I don't think double albums are good. I don't think kids have the money to spend 30 bucks on a record.' The two albums feature guest appearances from long-time pal Eminem as well as country-pop crossover queen Sheryl Crow. Kid Rock also made his big-screen debut in *Joe Dirt*, a film starring comedian David Spade as a mentally handicapped man searching for the parents that abandoned him, and Rock as 'Robby', the retard's romantic rival.

'I never said I wanted to be around for a long time. I always wanted to be here for a good time.' – Kid Rock

The first of the two albums recorded during 2001, *Cocky*, was released early in 2002 to mixed reviews and disappointing sales. In the meantime, the super-pimp has become a fixture in gossip sheets worldwide on account of his forth-coming marriage to Pamela Anderson. The media interest surrounding them has been intense, not least due to the reaction of Pammy's former husband, Motley Crue drummer Tommy Lee, who, despite Kid's claims to the contrary, is said to be less than delighted about the relationship. Rumours that a Kid 'n' Pam home-porn video is soon to be available have already been denied.

Slipknot – a nine-headed hydra of mayhem and malevolence.

DIE FOR THE BAND
Slipknot

'Our children have no direction. They're mutilating themselves with crack and meth and ecstasy. I want kids to question why and not settle for what they're given. I put myself on the cross for them.' – Shawn Crahan, Slipknot

Described by the UK's *Daily Telegraph* as 'the most revolting band in the world', Slipknot are a brutal distillation of the preceding twenty years of rock music. Their record company press release seeks to define the band's uncompromising sound and image: 'draped in [Midwestern psycho killer] Ed Gein style coveralls and nightmarishly surreal masks, touting a sound patched from the best parts of hip-hop, metal (and) violent LA style "new metal".' Slipknot are simply the heaviest, most dynamic act to emerge from the diverse melting pot of the nu-metal genre. A nine-headed hydra of mayhem and malevolence, the group combine a super-charged death-metal guitar sound with ferocious three-pronged percussive assaults. Heavily influenced by Slayer, the group prefer to distance themselves from the likes of Korn and Limp Bizkit, describing their sound as 'metal metal'. Live, Slipknot are a spectacle of non-stop motion, which regularly descends to the level of on-stage brawling between band members. On disc, the group are massively successful – their self-titled first album going platinum within two months of its release, while the follow-up, *Iowa*, debuted in the *Billboard* chart at number three. During their short career, Slipknot have amassed legions of committed fans, referred to by the band as 'maggots'. Voted 'The Best Band in the World' for two consecutive years, by *Kerrang!* readers, the group are enjoying unprecedented levels of popularity both at home and across Europe.

'Des Moines is kind of like a graveyard with buildings shooting up from it. It's a small place, 200,000 people, with the majority being old people. It's got the sec-

ond highest concentration of old people in the country. Try being a fifteen year old in that kind of puritanical, totalitarian environment. There's nothing to do at that age except rage! You're going totally nuts inside. I don't want to say it made us who we are but it played a part in the band's attitude.' Corey Taylor

Originating from Des Moines, Iowa, Slipknot were originally drawn together in 1995 as a grass-roots supergroup incorporating the cream of local talent. Des Moines is a drab Midwestern town ignored by most rock-tour itineraries, but with a small underground gig circuit of its own. (An exception to this was the night in 1981 when Ozzy Osbourne came to town, and bit the head off of a bat.) Into this environment came Slipknot. Originally a sextet, the band consisted of Anders Colsefni on vocals, Donnie Steele and Josh Brainard on guitars, Paul Gray on bass, Joey Jordison and Shawn Craham providing drums and percussion. On 4 December 1995, the original line-up made their live debut at the Crowbar Club, under the name of 'Meld'. The group performed a short set, which, according to vocalist Colsefni, 'freaked the hell out of everybody'. At this stage, the band's sound was different to the sonic blitzkrieg of the fully-formed Slipknot: as well as the all-pervasive death metal/thrash influences, Meld were heavily inclined towards the funk-rock groove of the Red Hot Chili Peppers. This interest in crossing stylistic boundaries was underlined by the band's name, coined in reference to mixing musical styles. However, some band members voiced their dissatisfaction with Meld, and a new name was derived from one of the group's song titles: 'Slipknot'.

The newly re-christened sextet saw out 1995 by heading into Des Moines' SR Audio studio to work on a demo. Producer Sean McMahon, urged to visit one of the band's sessions by studio owner Mike Lawyer, was impressed enough to describe Slipknot as 'the most original band I have ever seen in the Mid-West'. McMahon quickly arranged for the band to record a debut album at Lawyer's studio, and sessions began as the year drew to a close. 'It was a hell of an experience,' Colsefni recalled of recording the album. 'The song that went down quickest was "Killers Are Quiet" and it's eleven minutes plus long. One take.' The sessions were memorably intense, foreshadowing things to come. 'Recording the samples for "Killers Are Quiet" – one of the samples is me ripping duct-tape off Shawn's face. That was when I decided I was going to wear electrical tape on my face. It was very strange looking.' The sessions, as well as originating Slipknot's masked fantasy personae, gave birth to a nine-track mini-album entitled *Mate, Feed, Kill, Repeat*.

Mate, Feed, Kill, Repeat fine-tuned Slipknot's live set, indicative of their very loose musical direction at the time. While tracks like 'Slipknot', 'Only One', 'Gently' and 'Tattered and Torn' would resurface on future recordings, 'Do Nothing'/'Bitch Slap' featured extended jazz guitar sections from Donnie Steele and 'Confessions' had a lighter, funkier edge than anything that the band were to record subsequently. As Colsefni later explained, 'We did a little of everything that we collectively liked.' Despite having an album in the can, however, the band remained without a record deal. To overcome this, they self-financed the pressing of 1,000 copies of the *Mate, Feed, Kill, Repeat* CD. As with the intial recording costs, the band were compelled to remain at their day jobs to pay their way.

'Recording the samples for "Killers Are Quiet" – one of the samples is me ripping duct-tape off Shawn's face. That was when I decided I was going to wear electrical tape on my face.' – Anders Colsefni

Such pressures had compounded the intensity of Slipknot's early sessions. It was during the recording of *MFKR* that percussionist Shawn Crahan arrived for rehearsal carrying a clown mask he'd bought while shopping with his girlfriend. Donning the mask during the session, Crahan gave a relentlessly frenzied performance, attacking his drums with abandon. Attributing the increased intensity to his adoption of the clown persona, Crahan decided to wear the mask whenever he played. With vocalist Colsefni resplendent in duct tape and loincloth, the remainder of the band followed suit by adopting a variety of masks, each one bizarrely alleged by the band to reflect the wearer's personality and outlook. Guitarist Josh Brainard tried a ski mask and an executioner's hood before settling on a rubber bondage mask suggested by Crahan. Diminutive drummer Joey Jordison adopted a Japanese Kabuki mask, and bassist Paul Gray selected a startling pig's face complete with pierced snout. 'Masks have been around like forever,' Crahan the clown explained, appropriately enough, to *Circus* magazine. 'For thousands of years people used masks but a lot of guys out there don't realise that. They see masks as something you use to hide, but humans have always used masks in two ways: To hide *and* to express themselves . . . Our main goal is to express ourselves, our feelings, our music and therefore we have to take our personalities back – I wouldn't know any better way than the one we chose! The masks are a vehicle that allows us to transport our individuality.'

The spring of 1996 saw the first in a series of line-up changes that were to aid Slipknot's musical progression. First, guitarist Donnie Steele decided being in Slipknot was incompatible with his 'Christian beliefs'. Despite this setback, the band soon filled the vacancy with guitarist Craig Jones, who had previously worked with drummer Joey Jordison on Jordison's side-project Modifidious. In keeping with the group's new visual identity, Jones was required to select some appropriate headgear. After initially taking the bank-robber option and simply wearing a pair of tights over his head, he adopted a diver's helmet decorated with six-inch spikes – presenting an uncanny, menacing appearance, and a potential injury hazard to his bandmates. Jones is notoriously laconic, described by Corey Taylor as 'having that serial killer smell about him'. When questioned by interviewers, he often chooses to simply zip up the mouthpiece of his mask and walk away. As Brainard's eventual replacement, guitarist James Root, later observed of his bandmate, 'I kind of feel I'm doing a service to the community by knowing where Craig is from day-to-day.'

'The masks are a vehicle that allows us to transport our individuality.'
– Shawn Crahan

Shortly after Jones' arrival, the ensemble played their second gig at a local reggae bar named the Safari Club. Despite Brainard's description of the venue as 'a shithole', the club owners were sufficiently impressed to offer Slipknot a regular monthly booking. The band's brutal but evolutionary sound was further advanced when it was decided that, after the extensive use of samples on *Mate, Feed, Kill, Repeat*, new member Jones should move from guitar to sampler. Jones' interest in electronics made him a natural choice, but Slipknot were now short of the twin-pronged guitar assault necessary to their sound. This was remedied by the recruitment of a seventh member, former Body Pit guitarist Mick Thompson, in time for their forthcoming residency. At well over six feet tall, Thompson cut an imposing figure – heightened by his adoption of a Hannibal Lecter-style mask.

News of the band's live show spread quickly, ensuring full houses at the Safari Club. Within the space of a few gigs, the Slipknot stage show had become a provocatively engaging experience. Taking the stage to a malevolent mix of insane laughter and ice-cream chimes, the band's visual image had the desired impact – Crahan often adorning his bulky frame with a nun's habit, a ball gown, or even a Little Bo Peep outfit.

By now, Slipknot were receiving local media attention, particularly from *Des Moines Register* journalist Erin Kinsella. (Upon meeting the band, the disquieted Ms Kinsella found them in a candlelit room, chanting in a circle – whether it was a communal ritual or they were simply playing mindgames with the press, becoming as adept at making an impression offstage as on. 'Until playing live a couple of weeks ago, they had been living in virtual isolation since last fall,' she wrote in a ground-breaking article on the band, 'preparing themselves, writing new tunes,

2002 saw vocalist Corey Taylor enjoy some success with his reformed side project, Stone Sour.

hammering out new instruments. Their music covers every spectrum: industrial, metal, jazz, funk, rap, disco, country. The music is vital to really express themselves, but so are the costumes, they say.' Paradoxically, while the masks were said to be an expression of individuality, the identical boiler-suits were worn to merge every member into the group identity.

Slipknot's fortnightly residency at the Safari Club was interspersed by regular trips to the SR Audio studio to write and record more material, and winning a 'battle of the bands' contest organised by local radio station KKDM. This little victory earned Slipknot some additional free recording time at SR, as well as a place on

Much scarier with the masks on – Slipknot pose at a signing session.

the bill at the annual DotFest festival organised by KKDM. KKDM assistant program director Sophia John also came on board as a full-time manager. Taking more than half the band's stock of *Mate, Feed, Kill, Repeat* – featuring a cover depicting Joey Jordison bathed in green light, within a metal cage – she included it in a promo pack mailed to record labels and industry contacts. (The remaining copies were picked up by Midwestern distribution company Ismist. No further pressings of *MFKR* were made and the album, which the band regard as strictly a demo, has become a sought-after rarity.)

> 'We just want to make as many enemies as possible. We're just here to piss people off with whatever we can find.' – Joey Jordison

The growing buzz around Slipknot was increased by their performance at DotFest and a series of well-received gigs in Omaha, Nebraska. This period of growth was to be interrupted, however, by the replacement of Colsefni as lead vocalist by Corey Taylor – former frontman of Stone Sour, a popular local group who (prior to ther revival by Taylor as a side-project in 2001) never moved beyond cover versions and uninspired heavy rock, beaten by Slipknot in the battle of the bands contest. Continuing a policy of using the cream of Des Moines talent, Taylor was approached by Jordison, Taylor and Thompson on the basis that he was by far the most talented vocalist. 'The idea was to bring in Corey and have him and Anders have a kind of trade-off, Anders handling the harder vocals and Corey the melody stuff,' recalls Josh Brainard. Reluctantly, Colsefni agreed to this new arrangement, but ultimately decided to leave the band when his input was marginalised to the point where he was little more than a backing singer. 'At the end of the show,' Colsefni says of the night he quit, 'I made an announcement. I said this was the last time I was gonna be playing with Slipknot. I didn't tell anybody in advance. Shawn just looked over and jumped down and sat on the floor.' Despite the majority of the band wanting Colsefni to remain as a back-up vocalist/percussionist, he left to form a new band, Painface.

Colsefni's departure remained the cause of bitterness for some months, the departed singer accusing the band of replacing him with a more 'radio friendly' vocalist. Corey Taylor's more versatile vocal abilities and stage presence more than compensated for the loss of Colsefni, however. Adopting a leather mask – similar to that worn by the 'Leatherface' character in *The Texas Chainsaw Massacre* – to which the singer attached false dreadlocks, Taylor quickly became the iconic representation of Slipknot's visual image. He also instigated a change in lyrical direction away from the less brutal approach favoured by Colsefni. Drawing upon an unhappy childhood, Taylor (like Korn's Jonathan Davis) vented his pent-up lyrical spleen at his absentee father.

The evolving line-up was further expanded when a long-standing friend of the band, Greg Welts, was recruited to handle the percussion duties originally earmarked for Colsefni. As 1997 drew to a close, the Slipknot profile was further raised by an inclusion of a live track, 'Spit It Out', on a 24-track sampler of local talent entitled *State of Independents (Vol. 1)* compiled by SR Audio owner Mike Lawyer.

In March 1998, the most important single event in the collective career of

'Our main goal is to express ourselves, our feelings, our music and therefore we have to take our personalities back.'
– Shawn Crahan

Slipknot took place. Manager Sophia John made contact with Korn/Sepultura producer Ross Robinson and persuaded him to visit a rehearsal session. Robinson had been unimpressed by *Mate, Feed, Kill, Repeat*, but reversed his opinion after seeing the group in action, setting up a deal for the band with his I Am recording stable (essentially a packaging operation for the nu-metal scene, selling Robinson's productions on to the record industry) and agreeing to act as their producer.

Before work on a new album could begin, however, the group became an octet with the recruitment of a DJ, Sid Wilson. Wilson (who was born with an extra finger on each hand) did more than simply add audio texture to Slipknot's performances – adopting a military gas mask, he engaged in progressively more physical live antics, often leaping from his decks to engage in cathartic fights with Crahan resulting in everything from cut lips to fractures.

Bearing all the hallmarks of a rock behemoth-in-waiting, the band travelled to Las Vegas to take part in the EAT'M festival – a 'battle of the bands' on a giant scale, featuring more than 150 acts on fifteen stages. Again, their performance proved massively popular and attracted major record company interest that wrested them away from Ross Robinson's I Am. In preparation for their imminent signing, the band enhanced their visual image with the adoption of matching jumpsuits that gave a uniform look. This collectivism was taken a stage further with the allocation of numbers (0-8) for each member of the band – designed to subjugate their individual identities to the collective whole:

#0 Sid Wilson – DJ   #5 Craig Jones – Samples
#1 Joey Jordison – Drums   #6 Shawn Crahan – Percussion/Vocals
#2 Paul Gray – Bass   #7 Mick Thompson – Guitar
#3 Greg Welts – Percussion   #8 Corey Taylor – Vocals
#4 Josh Brainard – Guitar

In a further move to distance Slipknot from the 'cult of celebrity', each boiler-suit was embellished with a stencilled barcode bearing the catalogue number for *Mate, Feed, Kill, Repeat*: 7-42617-0000-27. 'We want to be unified by wearing one thing. So we're together as a tribe instead of one guy being richer than the other guy,' explained Crahan.

While a number of labels expressed an interest in signing Slipknot, Ross Robinson's connections as a producer to the Roadrunner label ultimately won the day. 'Mercury Records, 550 Records and Epic Records came and checked us out and they would freak out,' explains Taylor. 'We actually had a deal signed with Epic, signed and ready. Vince Bonham, I will never forget the prick-ass-bastard's name, comes and sees us in Las Vegas. We throw down in Vegas, we fucking destroyed. Vince, who's like, 50 years old, says, "If this is the future of music then I don't wanna be alive." We looked at him and were like, "Guess what? We are the future of music and we want you dead."'

> 'We could never have predicted the kind of success we've got. I thought we'd be lucky to sell 100,000 records.' – Mick Thompson

Mere days before the band were set to sign a $500,000 contract with Roadrunner, on 8 July 1998, Greg Welts was fired from the band. Welts, who had adopted the persona of a demented infant he christened 'Cuddles', had been a key part of the band's live act – as hyperactive and manic as Crahan and Wilson, he often destroyed sets and equipment during his performances. Due to ongoing litigation, the full facts surrounding his departure have yet to come to light – but Welts subsequently disappeared from the music scene, and is rumoured to be running a tattoo parlour in South Dakota with the amusing name 'The Ultimate Prick'.

After signing with Roadrunner, the latest recruit to the mutant army was found once again in the incestuous Des Moines scene. Drummer Chris Fehn was a friend of guitarist Mick Thompson, and had previously auditioned for Colsefni's new outfit Painface. Taking the vacant #3 boiler suit, Fehn arrived at rehearsal sporting a white-faced fetish mask crowned by an impressively phallic rubber nose. Restored to full strength, the group left Des Moines for Malibu, to record fifteen new tracks at the Indigo Ranch studios where they would work with greater intensity than ever before. Psychologically motivated by Ross Robinson, the band drew upon previously untapped reserves. 'We're a highly, highly aggressive band and very seldom do we meet people who are in the realm of our aggressiveness when we play as a unit,' explained Crahan. 'Ross took us into the recording room and was throwing punches at us. He was into it. Ross got up every day and worked out so he could be in shape to do our album.'

Recording was finally completed in mid-November, with final remixing scheduled for early in the New Year. However, the traditional pattern of events reasserted itself when guitarist Josh Brainard announced his decision to quit. Apparently bearing no ill will, Brainard departed with only his amp and waived any claims to future royalties. Like Colsefni, Brainard returned immediately to the local scene, forming a new outfit called Undone. As the band returned to Indigo Ranch for the final mixing, former Atomic Opera and Deadfront guitarist James Root stepped up to the bat. The six' six" axeman effortlessly assumed Brainard's guitar duties and #4 suit, but was not so comfortable with his bondage mask. 'The bondage hood was really painful,' Root later recalled. 'I played one show in it and it really sucked. It trapped all the sweat around my head and it filled my ears up with sweat and it pushed into my eye sockets and it was a real pain in the ass. So it was time for me to develop my own thing.' Adopting a white mask that gave him the face of a malevolent jester, Root took the band up to its full complement which, to date, remains unchanged. As bassist Paul Gray describes their evolution, 'We built the band that we wanted to hear. We added members until it sounded right. In the beginning we had the idea around the three percussionists. We got two guitar players, bass player, singer. We used sampling, so we got a sampler and a DJ. We built the band that we wanted to hear and see live. It was all for us.'

'A lot of times people think we're really contrived – like we sit down and have band meetings and decide what we're gonna do. We could never know that we were going to get a record deal. No one in Des Moines ever got a record deal, so it was never even a consideration. It's always been just to make ourselves happy. That's what's cool about it; it's honest. We could never have predicted the kind of success we've got. I thought we'd be lucky to sell 100,000 records.'
Mick Thompson

Slipknot's eponymous debut album was unleashed upon an unsuspecting world on 29 June 1999. Containing all fifteen tracks recorded at the Indigo Ranch sessions, the album was by far the most uncompromising heavyweight rock LP of the decade, and by far the heaviest offshoot of the prevailing nu-metal school. From the nightmarish opening samples of '742617000027' to the anguished finale of 'Scissors', the album reached unprecedented levels of rage and intensity. The experimentation of *Mate, Feed, Kill, Repeat* was replaced with an assured brutality so intense that it's not always easy to experience the entire album in a single sitting. The *MKFR* opener 'Slipknot' was adapted as '(Sic)', a hyperspeed reworking of the original. Driven by Jordison, Crahan and Fehn's precise and unrelenting percussion, '(Sic)' is a lyri-

Released in 1999, Slipknot, *was acclaimed by* Rolling Stone *as 'brutally intense and totally fucking scary'.*

cal attack on how the mass media controls reality.

Throughout the album, Taylor's vocals veer between the manic bellowing of 'Eyeless' and the subtle, sickly-sweet delivery of the melodic sections of 'Wait and Bleed'. The chorus of 'Eyeless' has its origins in a rambling statement by a drunk that the band encountered on a trip to New York: 'You can't see California without Marlon Brando's eyes.' Describing the meaning of the song, Joey Jordison explains, 'It's not necessarily about Marlon Brando's eyes . . . that song is about Corey's dad and how he doesn't know him.' The lyrical meaning of 'Wait and Bleed' is just as internally subjective, and much darker: 'It's about this guy that keeps having repetitive black and white dreams of himself lying in a bath of blood,' reveals Taylor, 'and one day he wakes up and he finds this dream a reality, but he doesn't want to believe this so he tries to fall back asleep and wakes up normally. So he basically "waits and bleeds".'

Musically, *Slipknot* is an innovative, multi-layered miasma of percussion, guitars, vocals, scratching and samples. Each musician makes his presence felt – from the thunderous guitar assault that Thompson and Root bring to 'Diluted', through to the dense soup of scratches and samples employed by Wilson and Jones on '742167000027' and 'Frail Limb Nursery' – but Slipknot are a true *gestalt*, very much greater than the sum of their individual parts. The dark, confrontational attitude of Slipknot's visceral manifesto was encapsulated by a slogan on the CD packaging: 'People = Shit'. Although their nihilism is summed up in the mosh-pit favourite 'Surfacing', which they have deemed a 'new National Anthem' – 'Fuck it all! Fuck this world! / Fuck everything that you stand for! / Don't belong! Don't exist! / Don't give a shit! / Don't ever judge me!' – Slipknot do at least share some of the trappings of more political bands: the use of slogans, the adoption of costumes that subsume the individual beneath the whole.

Two of the tracks on the original pressing of *Slipknot* – 'Frail Limb Nursery' and 'Purity' – were inspired by a *Blair Witch Project*-style website that recounted the story of Purity Knight, a teenage girl said to have been brutally murdered by an unidentified killer. The owners of the website, www.crimescene.com, insisted that, as the story was fictional, the character of Purity Knight was their intellectual property, leading to the withdrawal of the two tracks from later editions of the album. 'I still think that it's real,' insisted Taylor, embracing Purity's sorry tale with the eagerness of wider society seizing on an urban myth. 'See the thing [about] whether it's true or not – it's a real story that we read about, that fucked our whole world up.' (The deleted songs were replaced by 'Me Inside', originally only available on the *Slipknot* digipack.)

'Live, I give it my all. I'm covered in my own fucking puke every night, dude. I think after that I deserve a little bass fishing.' – Shawn Crahan

Slipknot was an instant commercial success, selling over 20,000 copies in the first week of its release. For a band without any prior mainstream product, or significant radio or TV exposure, it was nothing short of phenomenal – but, as percussionist Chris Fehn said, 'There's other ways to access a band than those bullshit mediums.' Although the buzz surrounding the group's live act was undoubtedly a key factor, Roadrunner's widespread distribution network was also influential – their 'street teams' distributing 50,000 promo tapes featuring 'Spit It Out'/'Surfacing'.

Slipknot were also included on the bill for that summer's Ozzfest tour, alongside their idols Slayer, and acts Rob Zombie, the Deftones, Primus and System of a Down. 'Ozzfest was what gave us the opportunity to play in front of all these kids who had heard about us,' acknowledges Taylor. 'What a great fucking way to come out, man. We were playing with some of our gods here, like Black Sabbath, Slayer and Primus.'

MTV also recorded some live footage at the Des Moines Lazer Luau festival (organised by local DJ Mancow) in late July, the performance of 'Wait and Bleed' used for Slipknot's first promotional video. It was a testament to how, as a live act, the group immediately connected with their audience. As Joey Jordison explained to MTV, 'The way I see it and the way all the guys in the band see it, when you go out and speak to a kid one-on-one and you speak his language, through songs about what that guy experiences day in and day out, that's what I think makes it. I think that a lot of bands go out, and even though they're speaking one-on-one, they speak a little bit over these kids' heads. I mean, this kid gets up at 6.30 and stubs his toe on the way to the shower and has his mom yelling at him and he has to go to school, and maybe he's not getting good grades. And his girlfriend is breaking up with him, and he has to come home, and then he has to do it all over again. He goes to bed and it's *Groundhog Day* for him, and that's what it's like for us.'

'We're a highly, highly aggressive band and very seldom do we meet people who are in the realm of our aggressiveness.'
– Shawn Crahan

'When we're comfortable is when this band doesn't exist, for sure. We thrive off the pain. You don't see any other bands getting up and playing beneath coveralls and still get the whole place slamming. But still, I can't wait to play all those shows ahead because this is what I love to do. Sometimes, man, I almost get tears during a couple of songs, but then I think, "Fuck it, I've got a mask on, no-one's going to see it anyway." Right now it just feels like it's the way it's supposed to be – us and the maggots.' Joey Jordison

The 1999 Ozzfest represented the start of a punishing year on the road for the Des Moines posse and their crew. As the tour ended, Slipknot headed straight back onto the road with Machine Head and Coal Chamber under the banner of the Livin' La Vida Loco Tour – the period that established their reputation for outrageous behaviour on (and off) stage. The cracked skulls, broken ribs and crushed fingers suffered as a by-product of Crahan and Wilson's leaping and brawling had already become an occupational hazard. Others began to indulge in their own unsettling onstage antics: Corey Taylor opted for inhaling the contents of a jar containing a decomposing 'spiritual' crow (as if Taylor had adopted a kind of witch's familiar) which allowed him to vomit at will, enhancing his already visceral performance. Tales of back-stage scatology and brawling were rife, as the band charged themselves up to produce the manic intensity necessary to perform.

Jordison, for his part, began engaging in the more passive pursuit of passing, un-masked and unnoticed, among the audience: 'I can walk through a bunch of people and they are all standing around talking about the show, and I walk by and they don't even know it's me, or that I'm in the band . . . I get to hear the kids talk and they don't even know who the fuck I am, and the fact that they say such kind words about us is such a good feeling.'

Slipknot's growing army of 'maggots' had in fact helped the album achieve gold sales in the USA, by September 1999, and a similar level of success in Europe. Newspaper column inches were grabbed when clown Shawn decided to take a crap in mortified 'shock-jock' Howard Stern's studio, and when multi-millionaire Fred Durst, threatened by the astonishing rise of Slipknot, dismissed the band and labelled their fans 'fat, ugly kids'. (This type of bitching is a staple of Durst's, having previously targeted Korn for abuse. Of course, the odd inter-group *fatwa* does little harm in terms of publicity.) Durst, who Crahan damned as a 'cocksucker', perhaps understandably failed to respond to Slipknot's collective invitations to 'step outside'. In response to Durst, Corey Taylor issued the following statement: 'You might have a lot of money and be famous, but the next time you talk shit about Slipknot and its fans, we will kill you.'

'The only thing I could see about it being nu-metal is because we're a new band. But our stuff is actually what they consider old school metal. I think nu-metal is like the Limp Bizkit sound. Personally, we have more of a death metal thing going, than a Limp Bizkit thing. They always have to put some kind of categorisation on it that a lot of people don't get. So, whatever. They can call it nu-jazz for all I care.' Paul Gray

At the turn of the millennium, Slipknot paid their first visit to Europe. In the UK, Wolverhampton's Conservative councillors expressed distaste at the band performing in their Civic Hall. The gig went ahead, but not without incident: nineteen-year-old Slipknot fan Lyndsey Pearce was knocked unconscious after DJ Sid Wilson landed on her following his leap from a balcony. A committed 'maggot', Ms Pearce refused to press charges, describing her experience as 'the greatest gig ever'.

Spring 2000 saw the release of a second single, 'Spit It Out', promoted by a video re-enacting scenes from Stanley Kubrick's film *The Shining*. Encapsulating the menace and horror of the Slipknot phenomenon, it proved too strong for MTV's stomachs and was withdrawn on account of the usual excuse of 'excessive

Slipknot guitarist Mick Thompson. The lettering on Thompson's fret board spells out 'Hate'.

Iowa was released in 2001 amidst a tumult of hype and anticipation.

violence' – essentially, a pastiche of the mad axeman melodramatics from the movie. On a brief return to Europe, the group paused briefly in their tour schedule to collect three *Kerrang!* awards, and set fire to their table at the ceremony. One proposed concert at Dublin's Point venue was cancelled following objections from the National Parents Council of Ireland. Drummer Jordison's response was typically direct: 'We were banned because the parents over there think we're going to warp the kids' minds. And we would have too.'

By now, the Slipknot profile was sky-high – they had been nominated for a Grammy award for their album, appeared on the cover of almost every major rock magazine, and their popularity led to *Kerrang!*'s production of a one-off 'Slipknot Special'. One reccurring theme throughout this extensive media coverage was the group's insistence on their ability to outstrip *Slipknot*. 'Wait 'til you hear our fuckin' next record,' Jordison insisted. 'It smokes our first album. The shit's twice as technical, three times as heavy.'

> '*There's so many different levels of pain. It's not hard for me to find things to rage about. I got issues and I'm not afraid of it. That's the beautiful thing. A lot of people like to hide their issues. Fuck that. Pain fuels me.*' Corey Taylor

The release of Slipknot's second major album, *Iowa*, was awaited by fans with the anticipation of a junkie waiting to score. The band first previewed its content during May's UK Ozzfest, where, resplendent in natty new black boiler suits, embellished with a goat motif and Nazi-style armbands featuring the trademarked Slipknot 'S', they performed 'People = Shit', 'New Abortion' and 'Heretic Anthem'. (The goat symbol, like the pentagram etched into Crahan's skull mask and the '666' lightshow used on stage, was less a theatrical version of Satanism than a provocation of fundamentalist Christian America – like the line in 'Heretic Anthem' that insists, 'If you're 555, then I'm 666.') Released in late August 2001, *Iowa* largely lived up to its hype by virtue of being heavier and more densely layered than *Slipknot*. A more unified work than its predecessor, the album's only weakness is the lack of any anthemic stormers in the 'Spit It Out' and 'Surfacing' mould – though the percussive onslaught of 'People = Shit', and the pounding 'Heretic Anthem', have become crowd pleasers, 'Skin Ticket' is another example of Slipknot's percussive force, reminiscent of Nine Inch Nails to the power of ten.

Iowa contains the Slayer-esque guitar attack and layered percussion that have become trademarks, and, like *Slipknot*, ends with its longest song: 'Iowa', the title track, is a timebomb of brooding angst that features evocative samples and an overriding sense of desolation.

Although much of the media heaped plaudits upon *Iowa* – with a procession of five-star, ten-out-of-ten reviews – others expressed their customary anti-metal reaction. *Entertainment Weekly* stood alone in giving *Iowa* a 'C-', stating, 'Apparently there's some cosmic law which ordains that every so often, a metal band emerge from the slag-heap to garner mass acclaim and platinum status. Slipknot, a god-awful goggle [sic] of Korn-fed mask wearing Midwesterners who identify themselves not by names but numbers 0-8 are the current lucky ducks . . . their second album, *Iowa,* has arrived on wings of hype and buzz. It's an almost unrelentingly brutal disc that, like so much of the nu-metal, often seems like a parody of itself.'

> '*I can't envision Slipknot in five years. How do you take something this extreme and keep pushing it? If any band can do it, we can, but after two or three records I think that's all there's gonna be. I'd rather break up than become a parody of ourselves.*' Joey Jordison

Iowa sold an immediate 254,000 copies, debuting at number three in the *Billboard* chart. Its release was followed by the Pledge of Allegiance tour, which Slipknot co-headlined with System of a Down. However, the earliest dates were delayed due to the terrorist attacks on the World Trade Centre and the Pentagon – both headlining acts subsequently dedicating their performances to the victims of those atrocities. While Crahan had formerly insisted, 'If we could shoot you with a gun while we were playing, I would,' and, 'We would blow up the stage and kill ourselves if we could,' the massacres on American soil clearly hit home. System of a Down espoused caution on the part of the USA's retaliatory response (and were attacked for doing so), but Slipknot turned their inherent rage outward against the aggressor – urging America to 'kick ass'.

System of a Down: Serj Tankian, Daron Malakian, John Dolmayan, Shavo Odadjian.

SIGNIFICANT OTHERS
The Post-Millennial Melting Pot

System of a Down
John Dolamayan (drums)   Shavo Odadjian (bass)
Serj Tankian (vocals)   Daron Malakian (guitar/keyboards)

'Do they call Bon Jovi "Italian Rock"?' – John Dolamayan,
System of a Down

System of a Down's second album, *Toxicity,* hit the top of the US album charts in September 2001, selling 222,000 copies – melodic and diverse, it was greeted with something approaching astonishment by the music press and surpassed the expectations of their fans. 'At the time the [first] album [*System of a Down* – 1998] came out there wasn't the interest in heavy music that there is right now,' described guitarist Daron Malakian, 'but we've sort of come in under people's radar: we get recommended to people by word of mouth and not necessarily even metal fans. I don't know who the fuck is still buying the album right now, but people are – usually people who also buy all kinds of other music as well.'

'I loved 'em – I loved 'em enough to sign them and produce
them . . . It's been beautiful to watch.' – Rick Rubin

Described by *Kerrang!* as 'the next big agit-politico's', SOAD already enjoyed a reputation as nu-metal's freethinking radicals. Musically, the band's eponymous debut was a highly original cocktail of styles, described by *Pulse* magazine as 'fuelled with rebellion and protest . . . diverse music which blends metal, rap, hardcore, jazz and Middle Eastern melodies.' Both albums have been produced by a pleasantly sur-

System of a Down's second album, Toxicity, *made the top of the* Billboard *chart in September 2001.*

prised Rick Rubin: 'I would never have guessed that they would have come this far, this fast. It's like they skipped a lot of the steps of growing up; there's a maturity about the writing that I wouldn't have expected when I first saw them a few years ago. I mean, I loved 'em - I loved 'em enough to sign them and produce them . . . It's been beautiful to watch.' Signed by Rubin's American Recordings in 1997, SOAD were similarly impressed by the production guru's affection for their band. As bassist Shado Odadjian recalls, 'he told us he was blown away, which blew *us* away – being eighties kids who loved all the rap stuff he came out with'.

'Politics is part of life, so we reflect that . . . We'd be lying if we left politics out, we'd also be lying if we let it dominate.'
– Daron Malakian

Tankian, Odajian and Malakian originally met at the Rose and Alex Pilibos Armenian School in East Hollywood. After the requisite period of rehearsal and experimentation, a line up comprised of Tankian (vocals), Malakian (guitar), Odadjian (bass) and Andy Khachaturian (drums), began gigging under the name of Soil. This nomenclature found little favour with some members of the band and Malakian suggested that it be changed to Victims of a Down, based on one of his poems. After some discussion 'Victims' was ditched and the band's distinctive name was coined. During 1995 the band established a niche for themselves on the lively LA circuit, which at the time featured the likes of Korn, Static X and spooky-core metallers Coal Chamber. In addition to their innovative musical style, SOAD set about distinguishing themselves visually. Jamie Miller, former drummer with Santa Barbara hardcore outfit Snot, was immediately struck by the quartet's frankly

System of a Down's Daron Malakian.

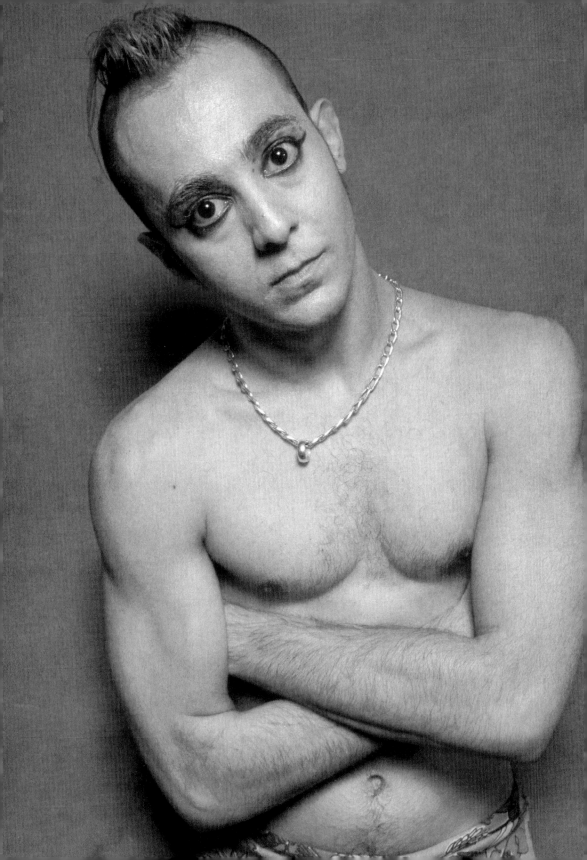

alarming appearance; 'Andy, their drummer had painted himself from head to toe in white paint, Serj had a huge beard and really long hair – he looked totally crazy. And Daron used to have really long braids and an Adidas sweatsuit. . . I was like, "This band is weird."'

Despite being slightly removed from the epicentre of the LA scene (Shavo admits to not even knowing who Korn were until after their first album was released), the band worked tirelessly to raise their profile through regular shows and a relentless campaign of flyer distribution. Shortly after recording their first demo, Andy Khachaturian broke his arm and was 'temporarily' replaced by former

Live, System of a Down are an exciting melting pot of diverse influences and boundless energy.

Friik drummer John Dolomayan. Drummer and band meshed instantly and Khachaturian, who had become frustrated at being confined to the SOAD drum stool, left to form the Apex Theory with former Soil bassist David Hakopyan. This reshuffle proved to be of benefit to all; with a settled line-up in place SOAD soon caught Rick Rubin's expert eye, whilst The Apex Theory were picked up by Dreamworks, releasing the excellent *Topsy Turvy* in 2002.

'We are *new* metal, but we're not nu-metal.' – Daron Malakian

System of a Down's noted political conscience is rooted in their ethnic history – they are of Armenian descent and have long campaigned for the 1915 massacre of 1.5 million Armenians by the Turkish government to be recognised as a crime against humanity, and for the US to cut its ties with Turkey. However, SOAD are keen to avoid being labelled a purely political band: 'Politics is part of life, so we reflect that. So are personal relationships, history, love, dope, anger, kindness, society, your body, everything. We'd be lying if we left politics out, we'd also be lying if we let it dominate,' explains Malakian.

The foursome have also been irritated by the casual racism of reviewers who focus solely on their ethnicity – one clumsily describing SOAD as 'Armenian Rock'. 'We didn't go out and look for Armenian guys,' insists Malakian of the band's (apparently coincidental) ethnic composition. 'We put a big focus on the Armenian thing, but it's not what the music's all about.' Like Slipknot, with whom the group co-headlined 2001's Pledge of Allegiance tour, System of a Down are also less than delighted to be labelled as 'nu-metal'. 'When you think of nu-metal you tend to think of these groups of bands – and I'm not naming any names – who tend to sound more close to each other than we do. We are *new* metal, but we're not nu-metal. That is somewhat like a trend and we don't feel like we're doing something that's really trendy,' explains Malakian.

Listening to either of their two albums bears out SOAD's originality and diversity: elements of the heaviest metal combine with a mixture of quirky elements, from folk music to virtuoso sections reminiscent of Frank Zappa. Live, the band's blistering performances have been described as 'terrifyingly good', with Serj Tankian's manic onstage persona a cross between Zappa and Jello Biafra. While it's not 'nu-metal' in the Limp Bizkit sense, the band certainly draw the hardcore of their following from that demographic. However, unlike less original outfits, System of a Down produce music that transcends any stereotyping. As Tankian claims, 'We have the openness to go anywhere.'

Linkin Park — not exactly a boy-band, but nowhere near as hard as they'd like you to believe.

Linkin Park

Mike Shinoda (vocals) Chester Bennington (vocals)
Rob Bourdon (drums) Brad Delson (guitar)
Phoenix (bass) Joseph Hahn (DJ)

'Our music reaches out in so many directions that there's pretty much an unlimited amount of cool bands with which we could play.' – Brad Delson

Formed in 1996, Linkin Park have been described as 'nu-metal's boy-band'. Appealing primarily to the younger fan with their upbeat, MTV-friendly rap-metal, plaudits from the 'serious' rock press were never going to come easy. However, the group have established a committed fan base and thus far sold around 2.5 million copies of their debut album, *Hybrid Theory*. Produced by Don Gilmore, best known for his work with Pearl Jam, the album has been mined for a series of singles – 'Papercut', 'One Step Closer' and 'Crawling' – which all made an impact on the charts.

Originally formed as Xero by Shinoda, Delson, Bourdon and Hahn, the LA quartet briefly renamed themselves Hybrid Theory before settling upon Linkin Park at the suggestion of additional vocalist Bennington. Named after Santa Monica's Lincoln Park, critics have suggested the choice of name and corrupted spelling were a cynical attempt to place their product adjacent to Limp Bizkit CD's, both literally and figuratively. Metal bible *Kerrang!* has been kinder, however, describing them as serving up 'industrial strength rap and rock melodicism with equal aplomb'. Linkin Park's chief dynamic is the trade-off

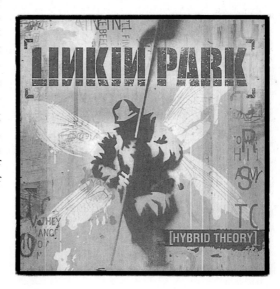

Linkin Park's debut album, Hybrid Theory, *was remixed and re-released in 2002 as* Reanimation.

'We want everything to have dynamics, but also a continuous cohesive flavor, so that you know what band you're listening to.'
– Brad Delson

Linkin Park – Brad Delson, Joseph Hahn, Rob Bourdon, Mike Shinoda, Phoenix and Chester Bennington.

between Shinoda's rapping and Bennington's emotive rock vocals. 'I think one of Chester and Mike's goals is to be as integrated as possible,' explains Delson. 'We want our sound to come across so that people go, "Oh, that's Linkin Park," not, "I heard this hip-hop part and now they're hitting me over the head with this rock chorus." We want everything to have dynamics, but also a continuous cohesive flavor, so that you know what band you're listening to.'

In addition to their catchy fusion of the lighter elements of rapcore, the band are characterised by their juvenile fan base. Keenly aware of this youthful demographic, the band have even been known to halt live performances to prevent the stagefront turning into an unruly mosh-pit.

Papa Roach

Jacoby Shaddix (vocals) Jerry Horton (guitar)
Tobin Esperance (bass) Dave Buckner (drums)

'I want to cause every emotion in people. I want them to fight, to fuck; I want to bring out their violence, their sadness, their happiness.' – Coby Dick

Formed by vocalist Coby Dick (aka Jacoby Shaddix) and drummer Dave Buckner in 1993, while the duo were still in high school, Papa Roach played their first gig at a school talent show. Over the subsequent eight years, the group have established a solid line-up and played nearly 500 gigs. Hailing from Vacaville in Northern California, a town best known for a correctional facility for the criminally insane, the group steadily built a local fan-base and released a succession of

Papa Roach – about to go global?

recordings – though, after their 1994 mini-album, *Potatoes for Christmas,* their first full-length effort, *Old Friends from Young Years*, would not be issued until 1997. Two five-track EPs – *Five Tracks Deep* and *Let 'Em Know* – attracted the attention of David Geffen's Dreamworks Records, with whom the quartet released their major-label debut, *Infest*, in 2000.

Papa Roach's lyrics are described by vocalist/songwriter Coby Dick as being 'about dealing with everyday struggle'. In keeping with the dysfunctional motif common to both Korn and Slipknot, Dick draws inspiration from his non-relationship with an absentee father for songs such as 'Broken Home'. 'We lean more towards hip-hop, punk and funk, and we also have a rock influence,' states guitarist Jerry Horton, 'but we're not really rap-core. The songs have a pop structure and they're very melodic, with a lot of layers and orchestration.' Originally influenced by artists such as Faith No More and Primus, Papa Roach also draw upon a broad church of influences ranging from John Coltrane and Duke Ellington to Metallica and Run DMC. The group have toured relentlessly throughout the past two years, supporting Kid Rock and Incubus as well as appearing at the Ozzfest both in the US and Britain.

Infest has achieved platinum status with its intelligent mixture of diverse styles. At the 2001 *Kerrang!* Awards, the group walked away with the statuettes for Best International Live Act and Best Video (for 'Last Resort').

Mudvayne
Ryan Martinie (bass)   Greg Tribett (guitar)
Matt McDonough (drums)   Chad Gray (vocals)

'The beauty of Mudvayne is that eventually people have to start from square one and abandon whatever they think we're going to be about.' – Matt McDonough

Obscured beneath layers of startling make-up and equally opaque lyrics, and featuring a motif based on the periodic table (progressive math-core, anybody?), Mudvayne represent the conceptual end of the nu-metal spectrum. The quintet were formed in Peoria, Illinois in 1996 and – other than replacing their original bassist with Ryan Martinie – have maintained a stable line-up. In 1998 they issued a self-produced and distributed album, *Kill, I Oughta*, which gained them a deal with Epic and impressed Slipknot percussionist Shawn Crahan enough for him to sign on as executive producer for their monolithically-heavy major-label debut, *LD*

50. Mixing Chad Gray's mesmeric and guttural vocal style with thunderous guitar, serpentine rhythms and a wide palette of samples, Mudvayne's sound is often compared to Slipknot (with whom they have toured extensively). 'If people wanna say we're a Slipknot clone – fine,' shrugs drummer McDonough, 'Slipknot and the make-up gave people an excellent first point of contact.'

'If people wanna say we're a Slipknot clone – fine.' – Matt McDonough

Musically, Mudvayne eschew the traditional verse-chorus-verse format in favour of experimenting with the structure of the song, before finally adding the lyrics. These concepts can be influenced by such diverse sources as the films of Stanley Kubrick, Terence McKenna's alternative shamanism or the life of serial killer Ed Gein. 'Our arrangements are so wacky. They have a sort of flow, but there's no form – every arrangement is different, every arrangement offers a different theme,' explains vocalist Chad Gray. Unsurprisingly, media attention has generally focused upon the band's outlandish appearance – at one performance, Gray appeared to be caked in dried blood and sported a five-foot long blue beard. 'It

Mudvayne: nu-prog mutants.

Mudvayne's fascination with science is illustrated by the use of a molecular model on the sleeve of their LD 50 album (2000).

doesn't necessarily symbolise anything,' McDonough said of the meaning (or lack of same) behind the mummery, 'and I'd really hate to see things like that taken too literally.' This type of nebulous evasion is typical of Mudvayne's ambiguous mystique – the band rarely give interviews and McDonough generally requests that security guards accompany him at all times inside concert halls. In defence of this, the drummer states, 'We are very careful about controlling what people see and know who we actually are and what we represent. For us to give too much away dilutes the ability for each fan to get their own handle on what we're about.' Despite their overtly pretentious overtones, the raw aggression of Mudvayne in full flow precludes any accusations of them being nu-prog opportunists.

'We are very careful about controlling what people see and know who we actually are and what we represent.' – Matt McDonough

Following the success of *LD50*, Mudvayne received a small amount of MTV exposure for the subsequent single, 'Dig', heightening the pressure on them to take their music-performance concept to a wider audience. 'We simply can't spend eight months on songs anymore and for the first time, I don't know how things are going to turn out,' complains McDonough. 'How do you escape for six months, write an album and still hold the attention of an audience?'

Static-X
Wayne Static (vocals, guitars, programming)
Ken Jay (drums)   Tony Campos (bass, vocals)
Tripp Rex Eisen (guitars)

Static-X: Wayne Static, Tony Campos, Tripp Rex Eisen, Ken Jay.

Heavily influenced by Ministry and heavyweight metal muthas Pantera, the jackhammer assault (reminiscent of post-punk pioneers Killing Joke) of Static-X inhabits the industrial end of the fusion milieu. The group was originally formed in Chicago by frontman Wayne Static and drummer Ken Jay. Wayne was originally a member of 'pseudo goth hippy' band Deep Blue Dream, alongside arch-pseud Billy Corgan, later of the Smashing Pumpkins. Relocating to Los Angeles, the duo added bassist Tony Campos and guitarist Koichi Fukuda, harnessing elements of heavy metal, industrial and techno to produce a sound that first surfaced, in somewhat muted form, on their debut album *Wisconsin Death Trip*. Due to the promotional videos for the tracks 'Push It' and 'I'm with Stupid', the album received mainstream exposure and ultimately went platinum in 2001.

> 'If people only knew what dorks we really are then I don't think they'd be into us as much.' – Tony Campos

The Wisconsin Death Trip tour was part of a mammoth 22-month sojourn that ultimately led to the departure of guitarist Fukuda – Static-X having little option but to record their second album, *Machine*, as a trio. Triumphing over adversity, the band produced a behemoth of an album, far heavier and more cohesive than its predecessor. 'The reason it came off heavier was just more of a conscious effort to go after the Ministry thing,' explains Jay. 'We were still experimenting while we were recording the first record,' admits Wayne, 'we weren't sure who we were yet. By the time we finished that and went on tour it was like, "Alright – we've established who we are and what direction we're going in."'

Returning to the road in support of *Machine*, Static-X enlisted axeman Tripp

Rex Eisen, formerly of New York rockers Dope, to appear with them on the Tattoo the Planet tour along with seminal metallers Slayer and Pantera. The group see themselves as distinct from the perceived nu-metal herd. 'We're tired of it and we're ready for rap-metal to go away,' opines Wayne of nu-metal. Like many other groups who put distance between their own music and the movement that, seemingly, no-one wants to belong to, Static-X's core audience is largely comprised of nu-metal fans. But, as Wayne explains, 'I don't want to be just like whatever's happening. I want to make records that are timeless. I can put on a Ministry record from ten years ago and it still sounds valid – that's the kind of record I wanted to make.'

Rammstein
Richard Kruspe (guitar) Flake Lorenz (keyboards)
Till Lindemann (vocals) Oliver Riedel (bass)
Christoph Schneider (drums) Paul Landers (guitar)

'The Germans have lots of endearing characteristics and, of course, lousy ones as well, and are, therefore, no different to the other nations of this planet.' – Paul Landers

Both musically and geographically, Rammstein stand alone. By no means a 'nu-metal' band in the accepted sense, the German sextet have built a following comprised largely of the same crowd who turn out for Korn or Limp Bizkit. Their nationality also sets them apart from the mass of groups currently vying for attention. Fellow Berliner Alec Empire aside, Europe has produced little in terms of exciting new metal music over the last ten years. (The British scene is comprised of comedy death-metal acts such as Cradle of Filth and Akercocke, or pop-rockers like Ash and the Stereophonics, while exceptions like Sikth, Raging Speedhorn, One Minute Silence, Sona Fariq and Violent Delight are relatively unknown.) However, Rammstein are far from marginalised – enjoying mainstream success in their homeland, with their every release achieving gold status.

Named after a German town where 76 people were killed in an aviation disaster, the group were formed in 1994 by musicians from punk, metal and folk bands on the Berlin and Schwerin circuits. Their 1995 debut album, *Herzeleid* ('Heart Wrong') was co-produced by a Swede, Jacob Hellner, who had previously worked with the metal-crossover band Clawfinger, with whom Rammstein gained a prominent tour-support slot. Combining industrial music on a dramatic, oper-

Till Lindemann: Rammstein vocalist, Olympic swimmer, pyrotechnic expert, and human barbecue.

Featuring tracks such as 'Feuer Frei', 'Links 2-3-4', 'Mein Herz Brennt' and 'Sonne', Rammstein's 2001 album release Mutter *has proven to be the band's biggest commercial success.*

atic scale, pounding rhythms and harsh Teutonic vocals with fragile melodies, *Herzeleid* was a huge success, taking up residence in the German charts for eighteen months and bringing them to the attention of maverick film director David Lynch, who (impressed by the group's 'intense sound') included two Rammstein numbers on his *Lost Highway* soundtrack.

1997 saw the release of *Sehnsucht* ('Longing'), the group's second album. It continued the fusion of industrial metal and synth-pop instigated by *Herzeleid*, and, partly thanks to cynical marketing (the album released with six different covers), sold in greater numbers than its predecessor. Towards the end of the year Rammstein embarked upon their first major European tour, selling out 7000-plus seater venues in Germany, Austria and Switzerland, and followed up by supporting seminal industrialists KMFDM. This period of intense activity saw the genesis of the group's fiercely pyrotechnic live show, where lead singer Till Lindeman regularly set fire to himself and drew blood by repeatedly smashing himself over the head.

The first cover version recorded by the band – Kraftwerk's 'The Model' – was greeted with horror by its composers: 'They think it's a terrible version. The worst they've ever heard,' revealed drummer Christoph Schneider. Their cover of

Depeche Mode's 'Stripped' is indicative of the band's pluralist influences, which also include the Red Hot Chili Peppers, Pantera, the Dead Kennedys, John Lee Hooker, the Prodigy and the Sex Pistols. Korn's 1998 Family Values tour exposed the band to a new mass audience and propelled them toward a Grammy nomination for Best Metal Performance. Rammstein also received a degree of unwanted publicity, when it was revealed that the Columbine High School murderers were admirers of their music. (The media caterwauling, however, fixated on a more visible scapegoat: dark pantomime-metal dame Marilyn Manson, who the young killers were apparently not even keen on).

Following another eighteen months of relentless worldwide touring, Rammstein released their third album, *Mutter* ('Mother'), early in 2001. With memorable promo videos for the tracks 'Links 2 3 4' (featuring footballing ants) and 'Sonne' ('Sun' – in which the boys get their bottoms smacked by a giant S&M Snow White), the group received massive TV exposure. 'We know we are very successful in America at the moment,' keyboard player Flake Lorenz stated. 'A reason could be that we are not copying American music.'

Amen
Casey Chaos (vocals)   Rich Jones (guitar)
Josh Hill (guitar)   Tumor (bass)   Zach Hill (drums)

'I don't want to be the President, I want to kill the fucking President. He is the problem.' – Casey Chaos

Presenting themselves as an out-and-out punk band, Amen represent the nu-metal demographic skewed towards the legacy of Messrs Rotten, Strummer and Biafra. Former Sex Pistols guitarist Steve Jones is particularly impressed with the band, commenting, 'Amen's far more pissed off than we ever were.' Originally formed by outspoken frontman Casey Chaos in 1996, Amen gradually picked up personnel until the arrival of Sonny Mayo and Tumor (from fellow punk ensemble Snot) completed the line-up. Chaos had begun his musical odyssey as bassist for reformed goth-rockers Christian Death. Following a stint with hardcore group Disorderly Conduct, he looted the title of their first album, *Amen,* for his new band, claiming, 'I wanted to be hypocritical just like America and how America likes to sugar coat their shit. I like to do the same thing. So when people hear the name "Amen", they automatically think it's something Christian or religious, when it's exactly the opposite.'

Amen's polemical live show brought the band to the attention of producer

Amen: before their record label problems and personnel changes.
Frontman Casey Chaos is pictured centre.

Ross Robinson, who signed them to his I Am label. Following pre-production work with former Killing Joke guitarist Paul Raven, the band entered the studio to record their eponymous 1999 debut, which created an underground buzz. The album was promoted with a series of violent and spectacular performances, often resulting in a catalogue of injuries to their energetic vocalist. Despite a litany of broken ribs and damaged limbs, Chaos refuses to take any safe options: 'I think the whole experience of seeing bands has become an equation – it's become an "entertainment experience" – you put in money and get a nice safe hour of enjoyment you can neatly file away. Amen is about getting more than that.'

Driven by Chaos's fiercely anti-establishment message, Amen's second album, *We Have Come for Your Parents* was described by Ross Robinson as 'the most violent record ever to be released by a major label.' Confrontational and aggressive, *Parents* represented a welcome antidote to the corporate alternativism espoused by

The cover art of Amen's We Have Come for Your Parents, *evoking the polemically-charged graphics of Crass and the Dead Kennedys.*

Limp Bizkit's venture capitalist, Fred Durst. Indeed, described as the 'anti-Durst', Chaos became embroiled in controversy when it was alleged he was responsible for posting Durst's private telephone numbers on the Internet.

While Amen's fan base continues to grow, the band are unlikely to become palatable to MTV – their visual motif being angelic, AK-47-toting schoolgirls, while song titles such as 'Piss Virus' effectively consign them to the underground. This matters little to the band, as commercial success is the very antithesis of what Amen are about – and therein lays their importance to the contemporary scene. Faced with a society that regularly attributes high-school slayings to musical influences, Chaos asks, 'Why don't kids kill more often? America is a violent society that is at war with what it is told to be and what it is. Music does not define society, society defines music. It's the outlet, a reflection. The establishment is just looking for someone to blame for the violence and uses music as the scapegoat instead of taking a look at what they, themselves, have created.'

During 2002 Amen have been beset by financial difficulties largely caused by the termination of their contract with Virgin Records. The band have been unable to independently release their third album as Virgin are insisting that they contribute $200,000 to cover recording costs before the master tapes are released to the band. This lack of funds led to drummer Shannon Larkin joining Boston nu-metallers Godsmack, whilst Sonny Mayo and Paul Fig have also left the band to pursue separate projects.

Praise God, it's POD!

POD (Payable on Death)

**Sonny Sandoval (vocals)   Marcos Curiel (guitar)
Traa Daniels (bass)   Wuv Bernardo (drums)**

'As a band, we respect the past, from soul to punk, anything you can think of that had emotion, we respect that.'
– Marcos Curiel

Whilst the very idea of a Christian nu-metal band may seem contradictory and incongruous, POD have transcended a maelstrom of derision to establish a burgeoning fan base. Formed in 1992 in San Ysidro, a Californian town near the Mexican border, the band have assimilated the cultural diversity of their environment into their music. They cite the likes of Bad Brains, Bob Marley, Run DMC and Santana amongst their influences, and it is this broad outlook, grafted onto an identikit nu-metal template, that distinguishes the band.

Originally a hardcore outfit formed by guitarist Marcos Curiel and drummer Wuv Bernardo, the band's direction was set for fusion from the moment that hip-hop fan Sonny Sandoval was installed as vocalist. Following the addition of bassist Traa, who hails from Cleveland, POD set about gigging where and whenever possible. Initial shows at parties, skate parks and small venues were soon followed by support slots with Green Day and the Vandals. A lack of interest from any of the major labels meant that POD were compelled to release material independently, via their own Rescue Records label. After six long years of relentless touring the band were eventually signed by Atlantic Records in 1998. Their first major label release, *The Fundamental Elements of Southtown*, went platinum and saw the band included amongst *Rolling Stone*'s 'People of the Year'.

'Music does not define society, society defines music.' – Casey Chaos of Amen

Released in 2001, *Satellite* expanded the band's audience way beyond the original cadre of hardcore fans and religious zealots. A visit to the official POD website reveals a degree of un-Christian pride in the various territories where *Satellite* has achieved either gold or platinum status. Their pride in the album is not altogether misplaced, featuring as it does guest appearances from Bad Brains frontman HR and legendary Jamaican toaster Eek-a-Mouse. Taking inspiration from rap, reggae, punk, hardcore and metal, as well as incorporating elements imported from nearby Mexico, *Satellite* paints on a canvas colourful enough to allow the listener to ignore some of its lyrical shortcomings. Despite being pigeonholed as 'god-metal' their imaginative recycling of diverse influences will to ensure the band achieve due recognition.

SCRATCHING THE SURFACE

In addition to those bands described above, there are other groups who deserve a mention. The sub-Beasties lunacy of the Bloodhound Gang, Machine Head's progression from Pantera clones to accomplished fusion-metallers, Alien Ant Farm's swift rise from obscurity to rap-pop flavour of the month, Canadians Sum 41's youthful fusion of punk, rap and old school metal and promising lesser-known groups such as Disturbed, hed (planet earth), American Head Charge, the UK's Lostprophets and Japanese cyberpunk heavyweights the Mad Capsule Markets are all noteworthy. Anyone with a keen interest in nu-metal and rap-rock fusion could reel off a list of bands whose omission is unforgiveable. To those bands and their fans, I apologise. Their day will surely come.

Led Zeppelin
Led Zeppelin (Atlantic 1969)
Led Zeppelin II (Atlantic 1969)

Black Sabbath
Black Sabbath
(Vertigo/Warner 1969)
Paranoid (Vertigo/Warner 1970)

Deep Purple
Machine Head (EMI 1972)

Jimi Hendrix Experience
Are You Experienced?
(Reprise 1967)
Axis: Bold as Love (Reprise 1967)
Electric Ladyland (Reprise 1968)

Steppenwolf
Steppenwolf (ABC/Dunhill 1968)

Blue Cheer
Vincebus Eruptum (Phillips 1968)
Inside Outside (Phillips 1968)

Iron Butterfly
In-A-Gadda-Da-Vida (Atco 1968)

Gil Scott Heron
Small Talk at 125th & Lenox (Flying Dutchman 1970)

The Last Poets
The Last Poets (Douglas 1970)
This Is Madness (Douglas 1971)

Funkadelic
Funkadelic (Westbound 1970)
Free Your Mind and Your Ass Will Follow (Westbound 1970)

Maggot Brain (Westbound 1971)
America Eats Its Young (Westbound 1972)
One Nation Under a Groove (Warner 1978)

Parliament
Chocolate City (Casablanca 1975)
Mothership Connection (Casablanca 1975)

The Jimmy Castor Bunch
It's Just Begun (RCA 1972)

Bootsy's Rubber Band
Stretchin' Out in Bootsy's Rubber Band (Musicrama 1976)
Ahhh...The Name is Bootsy, Baby! (Musicrama 1977)

Lightning Rod
Hustler's Convention (Douglas 1973)

Joe Gibbs and the Professionals
African Dub Chapter 1 (Lightning 1977)
African Dub Chapter 2 (Lightning 1977)
African Dub Chapter 3 (Lightning 1978)
African Dub Chapter 4 (Lightning 1979)

King Tubby
Blackboard Jungle (King Tubby 1973)
The Roots of Dub (Gorgon 1975)

Lee Perry
Super Ape (Mango 1976)
Time Boom X De Devil Dead

(On-U Sound 1987)

Jah Shaka
Commandments of Dub Chapter 1 (Jah Shaka 1982)

Scientist
Scientist Meets the Space Invaders (Greensleeves 1981)
Scientist Rids the World of the Evil Curse of the Vampires (Greensleeves 1981)
Scientist Wins the World Cup (Greensleeves 1982)

Clint Eastwood and General Saint
Two Bad DJ (Greensleeves 1981)

Yellowman
Zungguzungguguzungguzeng (Greensleeves 1983)

Eek-a-Mouse
Wa Do Dem (Greensleeves 1982)
Skidip (Greensleeves 1982)

The Clash
The Clash (CBS 1977)
Give 'Em Enough Rope (CBS 1978)
London Calling (CBS 1979)

The Slits
The Peel Sessions (Strange Fruit 1992)
Cut (Island 1979)
Return of the Giant Slits (CBS 1981)

Gang of Four
Entertainment (EMI 1979)

Don Letts
Dread Meets Punk Rockers

Uptown (EMI 2001)

Public Image Ltd
Metal Box (Virgin 1979)

Jah Wobble
Betrayal (Virgin 1980)

The Pop Group
'We Are All Prostitutes' -
seven-inch single (Rough
Trade 1979)
Y (Radarscope 1979)

Basement 5
1965-80 (Island 1980)
'Silicon Chip' – ten-inch single (Island 1979)

Bad Brains
Bad Brains – cassette (ROIR
1982)
Rock for Light (Caroline 1983)
I Against I (SST 1986)

Dead Kennedys
*Fresh Fruit for Rotting
Vegetables* (Cherry Red 1980)
In God We Trust (Alternative
Tentacles 1981)

Crass
Feeding of the 5000 (Crass
1978)
Stations of the Crass (Crass
1979)
Christ: The Album (Crass
1981)

Sugarhill Gang
The Sugarhill Gang (Sugar
Hill 1980)

**Grandmaster Flash & The
Furious Five**
Greatest Messages (Sugar Hill
1984)

Kurtis Blow
Kurtis Blow (Mercury 1980)
Tough (Mercury 1982)

Afrika Bambaataa
Planet Rock: The Album
(Tommy Boy 1986)
*Beware (The Funk Is
Everywhere)* (Tommy Boy
1986)

Shango
Shango Funk Theology
(Celluloid 1984)

Time Zone
'World Destruction' – twelve-
inch single (Celluloid 1984)

Run DMC
Run DMC (Profile 1984)
King of Rock (Profile 1984)
Raising Hell (Profile 1986)

LL Cool J
Radio (Def Jam 1985)
Bigger and Deffer (Def Jam
1987)

Beastie Boys
Licensed to Ill (Def Jam 1986)
Paul's Boutique (Capitol 1989)
Check Your Head (Grand
Royal 1992)
Ill Communication (Grand
Royal 1994)

Public Enemy
Yo! Bum Rush the Show (Def
Jam 1987)
*It Takes a Nation of Millions
to Hold Us Back*
(Def Jam 1988)

3rd Bass
The Cactus Album (Def Jam
1989)

House of Pain
House of Pain (Tommy Boy
1992)

Red Hot Chili Peppers
Red Hot Chili Peppers (EMI
1984)
Freaky Styley (EMI 1985)
BloodSugarSexMagik
(Warner 1991)

Faith No More
We Care a Lot (Mordam
1985)
The Real Thing
(Slash/Reprise 1989)

Slayer
Reign in Blood (Def Jam 1986)

Anthrax
Spreading the Disease (Island
1985)
'I'm The Man' – twelve-inch
EP (Island 1987)

Rage Against the Machine
Rage Against the Machine
(Epic 1992)
Evil Empire (Epic 1996)
The Battle of Los Angeles
(Epic 1999)

Sepultura
Chaos AD (Roadrunner 1993)
Roots (Roadrunner 1996)

Biohazard
Urban Discipline
(Roadrunner 1992)
State of the World Address
(Warner 1994)

Dog Eat Dog
All Boro Kings (Roadrunner
1994)

The Goats
No Goats, No Glory (Sony 1994)

Dub War
Pain (Earache 1995)

Primus
Pork Soda (Atlantic 1993)

Ice-T
Rhyme Pays (Sire 1987)
The Iceberg: Freedom of Speech…Just Watch What You Say (Sire 1989)
O.G. Original Gangster (Sire 1991)

Body Count
Body Count (Sire 1992)

Nine Inch Nails
Pretty Hate Machine (TVT 1989)
Head like a Hole (TVT 1990)
Broken (TVT/Interscope 1992)
The Downward Spiral (Nothing 1994)
Further Down the Spiral (Nothing 1995)
The Fragile (Nothing 1999)

Ministry
Land of Rape and Honey (Sire 1988)
The Mind Is a Terrible Thing to Taste (Sire 1989)
Psalm 69: The Way to Succeed and the Way to Suck Eggs (Sire 1992)

White Zombie
La Sexorcisto: Devil Music Volume 1 (Geffen 1992)
Astro Creep 2000 (Geffen 1995)

Rob Zombie
Hellbilly Deluxe (Geffen 1998)
The Sinister Urge (Geffen 2001)

Korn
Korn (Epic 1994)
Life Is Peachy (Epic 1996)
Follow the Leader (Epic 1998)
Issues (Epic 1999)
Untouchables (Epic 2002)

The Deftones
Adrenaline (Warner 1995)

Limp Bizkit
Three Dollar Bill Y'all$ (Interscope 1998)
Significant Other (Interscope 1999)
Chocolate Starfish and the Hot Dog Flavoured Water (Interscope 2000)

Kid Rock
Devil without a Cause (Atlantic 1998)
The History of Rock (Atlantic 1999)

Slipknot
Slipknot (Roadrunner 1999)
Iowa (Roadrunner 2000)

System of a Down
System of a Down (Columbia 1998)
Toxicity (Columbia 2001)
Steal This Album (Columbia 2002)

Papa Roach
Infest (Dreamworks 2000)

Linkin Park
Hybrid Theory (Warner 2000)

Mudvayne
LD 50 (Epic 2000)
Static-X Machine (Warner 2001)

Rammstein
Herzeleid (Motor 1995)
Sensucht (Motor 1997)
Mutter (Motor 2001)

Amen
Amen (Virgin 1999)
We Have Come for Your Parents (Virgin 2000)

POD
Satellite   (Warner 2001)

Soulfly
Soulfly (Roadrunner 1998)
Primitive (Roadrunner 2000)
3 (Roadrunner 2002)

Bloodhound Gang
Hooray for Boobies (Geffen 2000)

Mad Capsule Markets
Osc-Dis (Victor 2001)

ACKNOWLEDGMENTS

Rapcore was dragged kicking and screaming into the world thanks to the assistance, advice and guidance of some good people, without whom there would be no such book.

I'd like to thank my editor Paul, for enduring me with patience and persistence. Similarly, thanks are due to all at Plexus, especially my publishers, Sandra and Terry, who steered me towards the straight and narrow, and Chloe, who kept me organised.

Thanks are also due to my other half, Donna, for her support and assistance, Marco, for his unerring navigation, and Adam, for his logistical help. Finally, I'd like to thank my grandparents, Fred and Nin, and my mother, Maureen for putting up with all that noise for all those years.

Putting together a book such as *Rapcore* entails a wide-ranging exploration of the music media. Books that I found particularly useful and informative included: Batey, Angus *Beastie Boys* (UK, Independent Music Press, 1999); Cross, Alan *The Making of Pretty Hate Machine and the Downward Spiral* (UK, Collectors Guide Publishing, 1999); D, Chuck and Yusuf Jah *Fight The Power* (UK, Payback 1997); Davis, Stephen *Hammer of the Gods* (US, Boulevard, 1997); Davis, Stephen and Aerosmith, *Walk This Way* (UK, Virgin, 1998); Devenish, Colin *Rage Against The Machine* (US, Griffin, 2001); Furman, Leah *Korn* (UK, Plexus, 2001); George, Nelson *Hip Hop America* (UK, Penguin, 1999); Katz, David *People Funny Boy: The Genius of Lee 'Scratch' Perry* (UK, Payback Press, 2000); Kendall, Paul *Led Zeppelin: In Their Own Words* (US, Omnibus, 1995); Klosterman, Chuck *Fargo Rock City* (US, Scribner 2001); Light, Alan *The Vibe History of Hip Hop* (UK, Plexus, 1999); McIver, Joel *Slipknot Unmasked* (UK, Omnibus Press, 2001); Mills, Dave, Dave Marsh and Aris Wilson, *George Clinton and P-Funk: An Oral History* (US, Avon Books, 1998); Ogg, Alex *The Hip Hop Years: A History of Rap* (UK, Channel 4 Books, 1999); Potash, Chris *Reggae, Rasta, Revolution* (UK, Books With Attitude, 1997), Quantick, David *The Clash* (UK, MQ Publications, 2000); Rocco, John *The Beastie Boys Companion* (US, Schirmer, 2000); Savage, Jon *England's Dreaming* (UK, Faber and Faber, 1991); Simmons, Russell *Life and Def: Sex, Drugs, Money and God* (US, Crown Publishing, 2001); Small, Doug *The Story of Limp Bizkit* (UK, Omnibus Press, 2000); Vincent, Ricky *Funk, The Music, The People and The Rhythm of the One* (US, St Martin's Press, 1996); Watts, Chris *The Red Hot Chili Peppers: Sugar and Spice* (UK, Sanctuary Publishing, 1995).

The following periodicals have also been invaluable aids to the writing of *Rapcore: Kerrang; Kingsize; Metal Hammer; New Musical Express; Revolver; Rock Sound; Rolling Stone; Terrorizer*.

The world wide web has also been an invaluable resource, and in addition to those responsible for the numerous fan/official pages featured in this book, I would like to thank the webmasters of the following sites: *addict.com; all-tunes.net; alternativetentacles.com; artistdirect.com; artistwd.com; bandindex.com; earlpollution.com; furious.com; getmsic.com; guitarcenter.com; guitarmag.com; guitarworld.com; hiponline.com; horizonmag.com; iconofan.com; insidecx.com; kronick.com; loudandheavy.com; ink19.com; juiced.co.uk; loudside.com; metalindex.com; metalupdate.com; mudmag.co.uk; musicfanclubs.org; nyrock.com; obsolete.com; rockmine.music.co.uk.; rockonthenet.com; roadrunnerrecords.com; rocknet.com; sexnrocknroll.com; shoutweb.com; sing365.com; sonicnet.com; southern.com; spinalcolumn.com; studio-sound.com; thadweb.com; thei.aust.com; totalguitar.co.uk; totalrock.com; victoryrecords.com; voxonline.com*

Thanks to the following for help in research, assembling visual material and supplying photographs: A Deadline Production/Funk Attack, Inc, All Action, All Action/Roger Sargent, Alternative Tentacles Records Ltd/Reachout International Records Ltd, Atlantic Recording Corporation, Redferns/Avantis Pictures Ltd, Gavin Baddeley, BMG, George du Bose/Tommy Boy Music/Vibe History of Hip Hop, CBS Records, Celluloid Records/Virgin Records/Kris Needs, Def Jam Recordings/CBS Records, Def Jam Recordings/Columbia Records/CBS Inc, Def Jam Records Inc/CBS Records Inc/Universal City Studios, Inc/Motown Record Company, Electronic Publicity Management, Epic Records, Flip/Interscope Records/Universal Music, Geffen Records, Inc, Geffen Records/A Universal Music Company, Mick Gold, Keystone, Megaphone Worldwide/Island, Music Library, Paisley Park Records/Warner Communications Company/One Nation Entertainment, Inc/Archie Ivy Ltd, Redferns/Avantis Pictures Ltd, Redferns/Paul Bergen, Redferns/Grant Davis, Redferns/Mick Hutson, Redferns/Bob King, Redferns/Michael Lissen, Redferns/Hayley Madden, Redferns/Martin Philbey, Redferns/Christina Radish, Redferns/Ebet Roberts, Phonogram Ltd, Profile Records Inc, Republic/Universal Records, Roadblock Music Inc, Rydim Music/Zebulon Productions/EMI Records Ltd, Sire Records Co./Warner Bros, Sony Music Entertainment Inc, Sony Music Entertainment Inc/Epic, Sony Music Entertainment Inc/Immortal Records, Sugarhill Records Ltd/Sylvia, Inc/Jigsaw Productions/Kris Needs, The All Blacks BV/Roadrunner Productions BV/Roadrunner Records, The Rock Lists Album, Todd McFarlane Entertainment,Tommy Boy Music/ Polydor Records, Virgin Records, Virgin Records America, Warner Bros Records Inc, WEA London/Jill Greenburg, WEA London/James Minchin, WEA London/Greg Waterman, WEA London/ Neil Zlozower, Annette Wetherman, Westbound Records/ Nine Records Inc, Lili Wilde, Worldwide Management/No Name Management.